Improve Your Social Skills and Storytelling

How to Use Effective Communication to Manipulate and Influence –
The Secrets of Analyzing Body Language to Successfully Dominate People

Daniel Anderson

© Copyright 2021 by Daniel Anderson - All rights reserved.

The following Book is reproduced below with the goal of providing information that is as accurate and reliable as possible. Regardless, purchasing this Book can be seen as consent to the fact that both the publisher and the author of this book are in no way experts on the topics discussed within and that any recommendations or suggestions that are made herein are for entertainment purposes only. Professionals should be consulted as needed prior to undertaking any of the action endorsed herein.

This declaration is deemed fair and valid by both the American Bar Association and the Committee of Publishers Association and is legally binding throughout the United States.

Furthermore, the transmission, duplication, or reproduction of any of the following work including specific information will be considered an illegal act irrespective of if it is done electronically or in print. This extends to creating a secondary or tertiary copy of the work or a recorded copy and is only allowed with the express written consent from the Publisher. All additional right reserved.

The information in the following pages is broadly considered a truthful and accurate account of facts and as such, any inattention, use, or misuse of the information in question by the reader will render any resulting actions solely under their purview. There are no scenarios in which the publisher or the original author of this work can be in any fashion deemed liable for any hardship or damages that may befall them after undertaking information described herein.

Additionally, the information in the following pages is intended only for informational purposes and should thus be thought of as universal. As befitting its nature, it is presented without assurance regarding its prolonged validity or interim quality. Trademarks that are mentioned are done without written consent and can in no way be considered an endorsement from the trademark holder.

Table of Contents

IMPROVE YOUR SOCIAL SKILLS

Introduction To Social Skills...11
Social Skills - Living and Surviving in the Society........21
Manage Shyness..33
Improve Your Conversations 50
Build Genuine Relationships 65
Body Language..77
Stop Procrastinating 93
How To Dominate People 106
Building Confidence 112
Make Friends without Giving Up Who You Are 124
Conclusion.. 133

STORYTELLING

INTRODUCTION.. 137
CHAPTER 1: STORYTELLING AND ITS IMPORTANCE.. 139
Storytelling - A Time-Honored Tradition..................... 139
Stories, Storytelling and the... 141
Healing Process... 141
Storytelling - Skills of the Ancients for Business Success Today.. 144
What is Corporate Storytelling?...................................... 148
Storytelling - How Important Is It To Your Brand?.. 150
The Art of Storytelling to Create Powerful Brands .. 153

The Importance of Storytelling in Content Marketing.. 160
Why is Storytelling Important in Marketing? 163
The Power of Storytelling 166
CHAPTER 2: USING STORY TELLING FOR EFFECTIVE PRESENTATION.. 168
The Art of a Presentation 168
The Ws of Effective Presentation.................................... 173
What Nobody Ever Tells You about Presenting.......... 178
A Presentation Tip - Tell a Story 182
Present Your Point More Compellingly - Tell a Story... 185
Presentation Using "Signature Stories"........................ 188
Storytelling: The secret to effective presentation skills 190
Business Storytelling Tips to Guide Your Next Presentation 193
Best Storytelling Tips for Marketing Presentations 198
The Benefits of Good Presentation Storytelling.......... 201
CHAPTER 3: STORYTELLING FOR BUSINESS PURPOSES... 204
Stories and Storytelling are Good for Business.......... 204
The Incredible Art of Storytelling in Branding........... 208
STORYTELLING TECHNIQUES IN BUSINESS 211
Better Online Communication for Your Business 211
When to Use Storytelling for Business 213
Storytelling for Business - Getting Your Point Across... 215
Effective Marketing through Story Telling.................. 217
How Stories Can Rocket Your Profits............................ 221

Storytelling For Internet Marketers 226
Unbreakable Rules for Storytelling in Email
Marketing 229
Storytelling in Marketing: Engaging Your
Customers in the Brand's Journey 232
How to Use Storytelling for Business and Why It
Matters 236
Storytelling for Business - The Surprising
Benefits 238
CHAPTER 4: HOW TO TELL STORIES TO YOUR
OWN SUCCESS 240
Why You Should Tell Your Story 240
Tell Your Story - People Want to Hear It! 242
How to Pitch a Story 244
Using Your Story for a Stronger Audience
Connection 248
Methods on How To Tell Your Story So People
Buy 252
How to Tell Your Story for Your Internet
Marketing Business 255
How to Tell Your Business Story to Increase Your
Sales 258
CHAPTER 5: A GUIDE FOR PERFECT
STORYTELLING 261
The Power of Storytelling - How to Use It in the
Business World 261
Ten Ways to Become a Captivating Storyteller 264
Become a Master Storyteller in Easy Steps 267
Guidelines for Storytelling in Any Situation 269
Compelling Reasons to Tell Your Story 272

IMPROVE YOUR SOCIAL SKILLS

Learn How to Stop Procrastination through Improving Your Conversations and Fostering Genuine Relationships

Daniel Anderson

Introduction To Social Skills

What you are about to discover in this EBook is the most comprehensive and eye-opening content written about improving social skills. This is the ultimate guide that equips you from A to Z about everything you need to understand about social skills and how it can be improved. Regardless of whether you are an introvert who finds it hard to socialize or an extrovert who looks to improve his/her social skills, there are lots of surprising insights for you to learn here. I hope you enjoy reading this EBook and while doing so, uncover the secrets to improving your social skills and taking your life to the next level. First of all, before I take you through ways in which you can improve your social skills, let's look at the meaning of social skills and its basics.

What are Social Skills?

Social skills are described as definite approaches applied by an individual to carry out social functions effectively and eventually be regarded as socially acceptable. Your behavior and interactions with others are indicators that reveal your status in the community you are in, if you are likely to be a friend or partner, and more importantly if they see you as a future potential asset to a company.

Good social skills are an essential part of building rich friendships, enjoying yourself in public, and succeeding in your career. If you consider yourself an introvert, it can be hard to engage in conversation with people you don't know. Luckily, the more you practice being social, the easier it will become.

In practical terms, what are social skills?

- A one on one communication where listening is a give and take interaction and each party intends to understand the messages conveyed.

- A skill that is acquired through continuous learning. As you interact, you begin to learn the aspects of the personality of the person you are talking to. You start to understand the person as to where he or she is coming from, and you try to put yourself in his shoes as he relates to his past experiences. You can draw out impressions of what he is like, and you try to act in a way that is within the appropriate norms.

- Socials skills have two aspects - verbal and non-verbal. A person with excellent verbal, social skills knows how to say the appropriate things at the right time, can communicate freely and get the conversation flowing smoothly, He/She is capable of using the proper vocal tone and quality and able to convey the message intelligently and understandably.

While a person with good non-verbal skills knows how to use bodily movement at an appropriate time, your gestures enable you to convey your message clearly through actions. Your posture, your eye contact, your voice tone, and facial expression are non-verbal social skills. Please take note that too many gestures can overkill. Do not overdo it.

- Social skills are influenced by culture and by a

particular social group. A person's social skills are based on how he or she was brought up. Most often, our behavior is brought about by our culture. A person's social skills differ from one another. A kiss and hug on the cheek as a welcome gesture may not be a socially accepted gesture in some conservative countries.

- How you behave during interactions, how you put your words together, your adaptability to the environment you are in, and the way you handle matters at hand are factors that determine how your personality is judged. It is not enough to have a ready smile and feel confident. It's not about looks; it's not about what you know that draws people to like you. It is all about who you are, what you do, how you do things and how others see you that you are judged. Learning what social skills are will help you get the reward of feeling accepted. Step forward and be recognized.

Social Skill Basics

Navigating the social world requires a certain degree of social awareness. Improving social skills does not end when you are an adult. You are always learning and adapting, even on a subliminal level, no matter what your age.

Children, on the other hand, do not have the experiences that adults have had and quite often do not understand why they have to see, do and say certain things that they don't want to.

Even as adults, with all our worldliness and maturity, do not fully appreciate how social etiquettes have changed over the last few years. For example, there are certain times and places to use your phone, or how to converse in the multimedia world.

However, three things are certain when developing and maintaining your social skills.

1. Seeing

Seeing entails finding your social cues. Notice the context of your situation. Is it casual or formal? Are the people around you acquaintances, strangers of casual friends? Different situations call for different kinds of behavior. Good judgment is necessary when you are social seeing. Notice how people around you conduct themselves and monitor their reactions to various situations. Basically, by social seeing, you are subliminally avoiding inappropriate actions or reactions.

2. Thinking

The second of these social skill basics involves interpreting other people's behavior and understanding why they are doing what they are doing. It also consists of predicting possible responses and coming up with effective ways of dealing with a situation or person.

If you struggle socially, it is quite indicative when you misinterpret other's intentions and are not able to immediately come up with constructive ways to resolve any social difficulty.

3. Doing

This is about interacting with people positively. Quite often we know what we should do, but experience difficulty in actually doing it. We might want to join a discussion group, for example, but freeze up and feel anxious in the social context of the situation. We either find ourselves being very self-conscious or totally embarrassed. If you are not socially aware, you might also speak impulsively. It is essential to hold a conversation at least or join into one.

These three social skill basics are essential in creating and maintaining all the different social skills.

Being enthusiastic and loud might not be the best way to handle a situation that requires quiet decorum. Social skills are about having the ability to adjust your behavior and be flexible in any situation.

Social skills are defined in various ways but are a necessary ability to get along with people and maintain fulfilling relationships.

Are you a socially awkward person?

Should you embrace your social awkwardness in social settings? Is it just a part of who you are? Some people will tell you to embrace it, but I genuinely feel that it's important to try and overcome being socially awkward as much as possible, especially if you want to create a life full of relationships, love, happiness, and success.

Being socially awkward will affect your life negatively. It may not affect your online presence, where you can say whatever is on your mind without fear of hearing a reply and where you can delete any word or statement you make. But, it will affect your ability to form real relationships with family, friends, and co-workers, and it will affect your self-esteem, success, and happiness in the long run.

The bottom line is that when you are socially awkward, you feel awkward or out of place, and that makes all situations and events with other people more difficult than they need to be. Moreover, it can hold you back from going after things you want because, often, the things you want are through or around other people, which can be hard to face.

Therefore, I highly suggest that you embrace your social awkwardness as a part of who you are now and then find a way to improve your social skills so you can become less socially awkward. All the information you need to improve your social skills is in this book.

Are you not sure if you are socially awkward? Following are some shared experiences awkward people have. If you find that you relate to almost all of them, then you are socially awkward and need to work on it if you want to change your relationships and life around.

1. People Avoid You In Social Settings

If you find people moving away from you or avoiding you during social settings, then there is a high chance that you are socially awkward. People don't feel comfortable around people who are awkward and lack social skills. It's hard to have a conversation with them, understand what they are trying to convey, and feel at ease around them. This is true whether you are at work or in another social setting.

2. You Avoid People As Often As Possible

If you ever find yourself ducking behind something to hide from someone that you would have to chat with, or crossing the street to avoid someone, or quickly shutting the elevator so that you don't have to talk to your co-worker, or canceling plans where you will need to interact with people, then you are probably socially awkward. We avoid people because we feel uncomfortable at the thought of having to engage with them.

3. Dates Always Go Bad

If you find yourself offending or scaring off almost every date you have, then there is a high chance that you are doing things that are weird or looked down upon by someone who is looking for love. A lot of socially awkward people don't understand what other people are looking for or find unacceptable.

For instance, you could be talking over your date, ignoring their questions, saying offensive things, asking inappropriate questions, or acting in a manner that makes them think you are too needy or desperate. Without being there with you, it's hard to tell exactly what you are doing wrong, but it's easy to say that something is going wrong if all your dates never lead into anything else.

4. Romantic Relationships Don't Last Long

You may find someone who can look past your awkwardness, but after a while, they start to grow tired of your inappropriate behavior or inability to be social and have a good time. They will probably tell you straight up during your relationship that they wish you were more social and outgoing. And, eventually, when things don't change, they leave.

5. You Don't Have A Lot Of Friends

Friendships are hard for you. You don't make friends easily, and when you do, you often lose them because you are not willing to meet their friends or go out and do things with them. You would rather sit at home with them than go out, which is a friendship-killer because friends build experiences in life and bond over those experiences.

6. Your Self-Esteem Is Affected By How Others Treat You

If your self-esteem goes up and down faster than a rollercoaster while you are in a social setting, even if you are not talking to anyone, then you are probably socially awkward. It means you are sizing up how other people feel about you through what they say and do, and then letting your conclusions – whether they are based in reality or not – dictate how you feel about yourself.

7. You Overthink All Social Instances

Big or small, you replay the moments in your day where you needed to relate to other people, and you beat yourself up over them. For instance, if you talked for a few seconds to someone about nothing important, you may not be able to stop thinking about whether or not you were friendly enough or stop worrying about what they thought about you.

8. You Are Scared Of Being Seen In A Negative Way

Are you scared that other people are going to see you negatively? Maybe they will think you are not funny, annoying, ugly, too sad, too happy, too fat, too thin, not smart enough, or not witty enough. If you think about these things before you even get into a social situation and have said a word, then that is a big sign that you are socially awkward. The very thought of being a social makes you uncomfortable because you care too much about how people view you.

9. People Tell You That You Are Weird

If people are outright telling you that you are weird, rude, annoying, or frustrating, then there is a good chance that you don't understand social norms and are rubbing people the wrong way. While these people can easily make you feel bad about yourself, they are also being honest with you and giving you criticism that can help you become less awkward and more confident if you embrace what they are saying.

For instance, if someone tells you that you are annoying, then you have a chance to work on some personal growth. You may want to look at how you interact with others. Do you take the time to get to know other people? Do you act appropriately around other people? Do you say things that are off the wall and don't need to be said? If you can find answers, then you can begin to fix issues that you may be having in social settings that make you annoying and then form stronger and healthier relationships with people.

10. You Have A Different Impact Than You Meant To Have

You try to convey how much you like someone, and you end up offending them. Or, you try to make someone feel better, and you end up making them feel worse. If you always find that you are not doing what you set out to do, then that is a huge sign that you are socially awkward.

OK. These are the ten signs of socially awkward individuals. Taking them into consideration, this is the right moment to ask yourself again "Am I socially awkward?"

Social Skills - Living and Surviving in the Society

Right from the time we are very young, we begin to learn the basics in social skills, which are, learning how to live with, communicate with, and get along with the people around you. If you have siblings, those basic skills come into play quite quickly; sharing of toys and sharing a room with a brother or sister. As we grow older and begin school, those skills become even more important as you must now share your space with many more people. Children who have not been adequately prepared for such an event may find it difficult to adjust to this new society they have become a part of.

To define the meaning of proper social skills, you would have to consider the environment or society you are living in. What works in one society doesn't necessarily work in another; none-the-less, basic social skills are imperative to live a happy and enjoyable life among others in your community, workplace, and home life. It is, in a nutshell, the manner at which we participate and conduct ourselves within society; what is right and what is wrong pertaining to the society in which you live.

In order to fit into society, society expects each person to act in a manner that doesn't go against social norms. Being rude to another person, cursing in public, disrespectful behavior is all negative aspects of not having proper social

skills. The more significant part of most societies learn

these skills early in life, and they are carried over into their adult life; however, there are some who tend to go against the grain of society and lack the social skills that most of us don't even have to think about; we just know how to act appropriately. There are also people who have a basic understanding of this concept but aren't sure how to become better at practicing their social skills in public situations.

For Example, when employers interview people, they aren't just looking at their credentials; they are evaluating how they interact with the employer. They look for signs and ask questions on certain topics requiring a social interaction to see if the one being interviewed has a good understanding of social skills as to how they would handle a delicate situation. The lack of such skills could mean the difference in getting the job or not getting the job; one must be able to conduct themselves respectfully and adequately in the workplace and among others in society.

Having good social skills gives you an advantage in society; people are attracted to those who display proper social behavior and don't feel uncomfortable in engaging in conversation with you. Having proper social skills is simply knowing how to be respectful, courteous, and understanding what society considers as the norm.

Helping children learn social skills

Some kids seem to learn social skills quickly, but others can benefit from some extra coaching. Almost every child struggles with friendship issues at some time in some way, whether it's trying to find a buddy in a new school, handling teasing, or having an argument with a friend.

These kinds of experiences are very common, but they can also be very painful.

Considering the three processes underlying social skills — seeing, thinking, and doing — can help you understand where your child might be stuck and suggest ways to help your child move forward. For instance, during a play date or a trip to the playground, you might be able to help your child see more effectively by making observations that draw your child's attention to relevant cues (e.g., "Mike seems frustrated right now." "Scott and Abigail are taking turns on the slide.").

If your child is struggling to figure out how to respond to a social dilemma, you might be able to support your child's social thinking by providing insights to explain the other child's behavior. You could also help your child brainstorm possible responses and evaluate their likely outcomes.

Finally, you might be able to create opportunities for your child to practice "doing" social skills by role-playing tricky situations, planning strategies ahead of time for tough situations, or arranging appropriate activities.

For instance, children who find it hard to make eye contact may find it easier to "look at people between the eyebrows." This comes across the same as eye contact but may feel less threatening for children.

Rehearsing simple responses to common questions can also help anxious children get past deer-in-the-headlight moments. "How was your weekend?" "Good. I had a soccer game." "How's school?" "Good. We're learning about the Mayans in Social Studies." These exchanges are a good way to handle predictable questions.

Kids often make friends by doing things together, so an interest-related club, class, or team might be helpful. One-on-one play dates often feel more manageable than group activities for children who are on the shy side. Some children who struggle socially with their age-mates do better with children who are a few years younger or older than they are.

Continually experiencing social failure doesn't help children learn. Children who struggle with friendship issues need guidance and support so they can "get it right" socially by seeing, thinking, and doing in ways that help them connect with their peers. Getting lots of practice having positive interactions with other kids enables children to feel genuinely comfortable, competent, and confident in social situations.

How Good Social Skills Contribute To School Success

Well developed social skills are among the major factors which contribute to school success. Positive social and behavioral competence correlates with peer acceptance, teacher and parent approval, and academic success. Poor social skill and maladaptive behaviors in the classroom correlate with school failure, higher drop out rates, social rejection, and decreased self-esteem.

Social skills are very specific behaviors which allow us to behave appropriately in different environmental setting and which help us develop positive relationships with others. Most of us learn these skills automatically through observation and participation in family and school life. However, some children do not learn social skills through general, non-directive strategies and require targeted instruction in order to understand and use these techniques effectively. This is particularly true for students who have learning disabilities. signs of poor social skills development include, among others, classroom behaviors such as defiance, disturbing other children, and inadequate independent work habits. With peers, one might notice problems such as aggressive behaviors, bragging, shyness, bossiness, and temper tantrums.

It is important to listen carefully when school personnel suggests that your child has peer relation difficulties or problem behaviors in the classroom. Some public school systems have short term counseling programs which offer social skills training in small groups for students who are at risk. However, many do not, and parents should be aware that they serve as the child's first teacher in the area of social skills development. Research indicates that social skills can be improved if specifically taught and practiced in a variety of environmental settings. The mall, restaurant, baseball field, and Grandma's house can all serve as teaching opportunities for the concerned parent. Natural settings can provide powerful reinforcement of appropriate behaviors which increases the likelihood of those behaviors being used in the future.

Thorough observation will determine whether your child is lacking a specific skill or is unable to use a known skill effectively. If lacking the skill, such as starting a conversation or entering a group, parents can help through the use of specific instruction, practice, and feedback. If the child knows the skill or behavior and is not applying it, the parent can help by developing a behavior plan which provides opportunities for practice and reinforcement of the desired behaviors, while reducing the occurrence of undesirable or maladaptive behaviors. an example of the latter is using good social problem-solving skills instead of engaging in temper tantrums or aggression towards peers.

Learning good social skills is a lengthy developmental process. Changing existing patterns of social interactions is often a complicated task. But good social and behavioral skills are critical indicators of children's later social, occupational, and psychological adjustment. Parents can help by intervening early when problems begin to arise. Skills which are taught explicitly in a variety of natural settings are frequently learned faster and used more consistently across settings. By teaching social skills, parents are providing the child with life skills which will be beneficial in the classroom and the word of work beyond.

How Good Social Skills Contribute to Business Success

Strong social skills are the difference between a good business person and a great one. Yet in business, the importance of social skills are often overlooked and neglected.

Universities and business schools do not formally teach social skills in their curriculum. It is expected the "soft skills" you need to interact effectively with other team members will be learned on-the-job or through corporate training initiatives.

However, when companies and human resource departments choose corporate training for their employees, they often prefer to invest in developing their employee's technical skill rather than their interpersonal or social skills.

Technical skill is important. It allows you to complete the tasks required for your job. However technical skill alone will not make a great business person.

A great business person will always go one step further and strive for the rare combination of technical plus social skill. They understand that by improving their ability to interact with other team members and clients, they can get the job done faster, more efficiently and cost-effectively.

In essence, by having a strong level of social skill, a higher level than your peers, you can increase the amount of value you add to the company. For employees, this could mean more promotions. For entrepreneurs, this could mean more clients.

As an Author in this niche, I create books like this for professionals who want to improve their social skills. Specifically, they want to know how to project more confidence in business, how to start and continue a conversation, and how to show their professional competence and worth.

Mastering these skills is the difference between a good business person and a great one.

In this section, I want to share with you 22 reasons why as a professional or entrepreneur, you need a strong level of social skills in business.

1. Social skills help you give a good first impression because you know how to present yourself positively and form a connection with others.

2. Social skills help you start a conversation with somebody new in your office which can lead to better relations with your coworkers and a happier work environment.

3. Social skills help you start a conversation with a potential client which can lead to increased sales.

4. Social skills help you identify the right outfit to wear in the office and at business events so you establish the professional image you want to be known for.

5. Social skills help you walk into a networking event with poise and confidence because you know the right body language to use.

6. Social skills help you choose who to talk with at a networking event so you can form the right connections in business.

7. Social skills help you connect better with your coworkers, clients, and boss because you know how to hold conversations and interact positively with others.

8. Social skills help you to get others to know, like and trust you because you know the exact steps to build each element.

9. Social skills help you build a leadership reputation because you will look and feel more comfortable

and confident in business situations.

10. Social skills help you build a strong professional brand because you know how to establish a consistently high level of presentation and interaction with others.

11. Social skills help you interact politely and professionally on social media and help you avoid damage to your professional reputation.

12. Social skills help you deal with conversation pitfalls such as an interrupter or a conversation hog.

13. Social skills help you remember and use names in conversation which will, in turn, help others to like you.

14. Social skills help you offer the right handshake for business and as a result, convey the right message to others.

15. Social skills help you exchange business cards with respect so you make that person feel important and appreciated.

16. Social skills help you understand the hierarchy of your company and the chain of command, which will help you navigate the corporate environment.

17. Social skills help you understand the dangers of extreme levels of know, like and trust so you can avoid damaging your professional reputation.

18. Social skills help you prepare for networking events so you can approach each networking event with strategy, focus, and fewer nerves.

19. Social skills help you work more efficiently and effectively in a team, leading to a more harmonious and happier work environment.
20. Social skills boost your team's productivity and therefore help your business become more profitable.
21. Social skills help entrepreneurs connect better with clients, leading to more contracts and increased profits.
22. Social skills will make you feel more comfortable in business situations (because you know what to do), and as a result, more confident.

As a high-achieving professional or entrepreneur, which reason resonates with you the most?

How the Seduction Community Is Screwing Up Your Social Skills

When most guys join the seduction community, they are on mission to improve their dating skills with women. Unfortunately, there "side effects" to joining the community that most of the gurus don't tell you about in the fine print. While most guys join with the seduction community sincere desire to improve their social skills, the fact of the matter is there is a very strong correlation between joining the seduction community and adopting weird behaviors. I'm going to talk about some of the side effects of the seduction community in this section.

1. Female Validation Addiction

The first side effect of the seduction community is that

you get addicted to getting validation from girls. This, of course, doesn't seem like a big deal when you're out sarging for months, but when you finally chill out and build a social circle, people get this weird vibe. Most people can't put words to it, but it's the vibe of, you constantly trying to manipulate women, even when you don't even like them when a normal guy would just be relaxed.

Guys become addicted to the validation of women. I had a friend who used to frown upon guys who drank and smoked weed in order to "feel good" until he realized that he got to a point where unless he made out with one or two women when he went out, he would consider that a bad night.

Doesn't anyone else see how unhealthy thinking like this is?

2. Pickup Skills Don't Equal Social Skills

Think of it like this, in tenth-grade geometry, I learned that

a square is a rectangle, but a rectangle is not a square. In the real world, pick up skills equal social skills, but social skills do not equally pick up skills. Social skills are a much broader concept. Knowing how to seduce a woman, unfortunately, will not solve your life's problems.

A common symptom that I've seen and heard from other guys on campus, is that after joining the seduction community, they have a very hard time making friends with guys. Why is this occurring? Because the seduction community doesn't cover a chapter on how to be a chill guy (although several people teach how to steal a cool guy's girlfriend). This has been a big sticking point for guys, and I think it's evidence of weak overall social skills.

3. Skewed Beliefs About Women

The seduction community also pumps some unbelievably skewed beliefs about women. While it is true that women are sexual creatures. The seduction community has promoted the idea that women are into flings with guys that they just met and don't know. I think this is the exception, not the rule.

I think that outside of the cold approach scene, where 99% of everyone else gets laid when a woman is attracted to a guy, she almost universally considers the future implications of hooking up with this guy. More often than not, she would rather have a single commitment than a random fling.

Within a social circle setting, this dynamic becomes much more obvious. Sometimes the courtship spans out over long periods of time simply due to logistics. It's the PUA nerd who's read too many eBooks, who tries to force the close on day three because he thinks it MUST happen then. This is not strictly true in the social circle game. In cold approach, her attraction for you evaporates like a vapor. In social circle game, your attraction is static, because your value is static.

My biggest "ah ha" was that social skills are bigger and more important than picking up skills. A guy who is high status, and has many high-status friends who are both male and female, typically does not have too much trouble getting a date. He doesn't need to spend thousands of hours listening to programs and cold approaching night after night. He also does not have any of the weird side effects that come from being stuck in the seduction community mindset for too long. He is chill, he is fun, he is dominant, he is social.

Manage Shyness

Are you shy and self-conscious in social situations? Do you feel isolated and lonely, but unsure how to connect with others? You may feel like you're the only one, but the truth is that lots of people struggle with shyness and social insecurity. No matter how awkward or nervous you feel in the company of others, you can learn to silence self-critical thoughts, boost your self-esteem, and become more confident in your interactions with others. You don't have to change your personality, but by learning new skills and adopting a different outlook you can overcome your fears and build rewarding friendships.

Do you need help dealing with shyness and loneliness?

As humans, we're meant to be social creatures. Having friends makes us happier and healthier—in fact, being socially connected is key to our mental and emotional health. Yet many of us are shy and socially introverted. We feel awkward around unfamiliar people, unsure of what to say, or worried about what others might think of us. This can cause us to avoid social situations, cut ourselves off from others, and gradually become isolated and lonely.

Loneliness is a common problem among people of all ages and backgrounds, and yet it's something that most of us hesitate to admit. But loneliness is nothing to feel ashamed about. Sometimes, it's a result of external circumstances: you've moved to a new area, for example. In such cases, there are lots of steps you can take to meet new people and turn acquaintances into friends.

But what if you're struggling with shyness, social insecurity, or a long-standing difficulty making friends? The truth is that none of us are born with social skills. They're things we learn over time—and the good news is that you can learn them, too. Whatever your age or situation, you can learn to overcome shyness or social awkwardness, banish loneliness, and enjoy strong, fulfilling friendships.

Here are a few questions you should answer before you continue reading...

Are shyness and insecurity a problem for you?

Are you afraid of looking stupid in social situations?

Do you worry a lot about what others think of you?

Do you frequently avoid social situations?

Do other people seem to have a lot more fun than you do in social situations?

Do you assume it's your fault when someone rejects you or seems uninterested?

Is it hard for you to approach people or join in conversations?

After spending time with others, do you tend to dwell on and criticize your "performance?"

Do you often feel bad about yourself after socializing?

If you answered "yes" to these questions, this section of this ebook can help.

Tackling social insecurity and fear

When it comes to shyness and social awkwardness, the things we tell ourselves make a huge difference. Here are some common thinking patterns that can undermine your confidence and fuel social insecurity:

- Believing that you're boring, unlikeable, or weird.
- Believing that other people are evaluating and judging you in social situations.
- Believing that you'll be rejected and criticized if you make a social mistake.
- Believing that being rejected or socially embarrassed would be awful and devastating.
- Believing that what others think about you defines who you are.

If you believe these things, it's no wonder social situations seem terrifying.

People aren't thinking about you — at least not to the degree that you think. Most people are caught up in their own lives and concerns. Just like you're thinking about yourself and your own social concerns, other people are thinking about themselves. They're not spending their free time judging you. So stop wasting time worrying about what others think of you.

Many other people feel just as awkward and nervous as you do. When you're socially anxious, it can seem as though everyone else is an extrovert brimming with self-confidence. But that's not the case. Some people are better at hiding it than others, but there are many introverted people out there struggling with the same self-doubts as you are. The next person you speak to is just as likely to be worried about what you think of them!

People are much more tolerant than you think. In your mind, the very idea of doing or saying something embarrassing in public is horrifying. You're sure that everyone will judge you. But in reality, it's very unlikely that people are going to make a big deal over a social faux pas. Everyone has done it at some point so most will just ignore it and move on.

Learning to accept yourself

When you start realizing that people are NOT scrutinizing and judging your every word and deed, you'll automatically feel less nervous socially. But that still leaves the way you feel about yourself. All too often, we're our own worst critics. We're hard on ourselves in a way we'd never be to strangers—let alone the people we care about.

Learning to accept yourself doesn't happen overnight—it requires changing your thinking.

You don't have to be perfect to be liked. In fact, our imperfections and quirks can be endearing. Even our weaknesses can bring us closer to others. When someone is honest and open about their vulnerabilities, it's a bonding experience—especially if they're able to laugh at themselves. If you can cheerfully accept your awkwardness and imperfections, you'll likely find that others will, too. They may even like you better for it!

It's okay to make mistakes. Everyone makes mistakes; it's part of being human. So give yourself a break when you mess up. Your value doesn't come from being perfect. If you find self-compassion difficult, try to look at your own mistakes as you would those of a friend. What would you tell your friend? Now follow your own advice.

Your negative self-evaluations don't necessarily reflect reality. In fact, they probably don't, especially if you:

- Call yourself names, such as "pathetic," "worthless," "stupid," etc.

- Beat yourself up with all the things you "should" or "shouldn't" have done.

- Make sweeping generalizations based on a specific event. For example, if something didn't go as planned, you tell yourself that you'll never get things right, you're a failure, or you always screw up.

When you're thinking such distorted thoughts, it's important to pause and consciously challenge them.

Pretend you're an impartial third-party observer, then ask yourself if there are other ways of viewing the situation.

Give up Shyness and Build social skills one step at a time.

Giving up shyness to improve social skills requires

practice. Just as you wouldn't expect to become good on the guitar without some effort, don't expect to become comfortable socially without putting in the time. That said, you can start small. Take baby steps towards being more confident and social, then build on those successes.

You should always:

- Smile at someone you pass on the street (No, you're not mad. Smiles....).
- Compliment someone you encounter during your day.
- Ask someone a casual question (at a restaurant, for example: "Have you been here before? How's the steak?").
- Start a conversation with a friendly cashier, receptionist, waiter, or salesperson.

How to face your biggest social fears

When it comes to the things that really scare us, you want to face your fears in a gradual way, starting with situations that are slightly stressful and building up to more anxiety-provoking scenarios. Think of it as a stepladder, with each rung a little more stressful than the last. Don't move on to the next step until you've had a positive experience with the step below. For example, if you're shy, and talking to new people at parties makes you extremely anxious, here is a stepladder you could use:

- Go to a party and smile at a few people.
- Go to a party and ask a simple question (e.g. "Do you know what time it is?"). Once they've

answered, politely thank them and then excuse yourself. The key is to make the interaction short and sweet.

- Ask a friend to introduce you to someone at the party and help facilitate a short conversation.

- Pick someone at the party who seems friendly and approachable. Introduce yourself.

- Identify a non-intimidating group of people at the party and approach them. You don't need to make a big entrance. Just join the group and listen to the conversation. Make a comment or two if you'd like, but don't put too much pressure on yourself.

- Join another friendly, approachable group. This time, try to participate a bit more in the conversation.

More tips for Dealing with Shyness

- Fake it till you make it. Acting as if you're confident can make you feel more confident.

- Focus externally, not internally. Instead of worrying about how you're coming across or what you're going to say, switch your focus from yourself to the other person. You'll live more in the moment and you'll feel less self-conscious.

- Laugh at yourself. If you do something embarrassing, use humor to put things in perspective. Laugh, learn, and move on.

- Do things to help others or brighten another person's day. It can be something as small as a compliment or smile. When you spread positivity, you'll feel better about yourself.

Tips for Starting a Conversation with Someone New

Some people seem to instinctively know how to start a conversation with anyone, in any place. If you're not one of these lucky types, these tips will help you start talking when you first meet someone:

Here are some easy ways to engage in conversation with someone new:

- Remark on the surroundings or occasion. If you're at a party, for example, you could comment on the venue, the catering, or the music in a positive way. "I love this song," "The food's great. Have you tried the chicken?"

- Ask an open-ended question, one that requires more than just a yes or no answer. Adhere to the journalist's credo and ask a question that begins with one of the 5 W's (or 1 H): who, where, when, what, why, or how. For example, "Who do you know here?" "Where do you normally go on a Friday?" "When did you move here?" "What keeps you busy?" "Why did you decide to become a vegetarian?" "How is the wine?" Most people enjoy talking about themselves, so asking a question is a good way to get a conversation started.

- Use a compliment. For example, "I really like your purse, can I ask where you got it?" or "You look like you've done this before, can you tell me where I have to sign in?"

- Note anything you have in common and ask a follow-up question. "I play golf as well, what's your favorite local course?" "My daughter went to that school, too, how does your son like it?"

- Keep the conversation going with small talk. Don't say something that's obviously provocative and avoid heavy subjects such as politics or religion. Stick to light subjects like the weather, surroundings, and anything you have in common such as school, movies, or sports teams.

- Listen effectively. Listening is not the same as waiting for your turn to talk. You can't concentrate on what someone's saying if you're forming what you're going to say next. One of the keys to effective communication is to focus fully on the speaker and show interest in what's being said. Nod occasionally, smile at the person and make sure your posture is open and inviting. Encourage the speaker to continue with small verbal cues like "yes" or "uh huh."

What to do when you get tired of social situations

There's a common misconception that introverts aren't social. In fact, introverts can be just as social as extroverts. The difference between the two is that introverts lose energy when they're around people and recharge by spending time alone, while extroverts gain energy by spending time with other people.

What this means is that even socially confident introverts will feel tired after a lot of socializing. It doesn't mean there's anything wrong with you or that you're incapable of having a fulfilling social life. You just need to understand your limits and plan accordingly.

- Don't overcommit. It's okay to turn down social invitations because you need a break or schedule downtime after socializing. After a fun Saturday out with friends, for example, you may need to spend Sunday alone to rest and recharge.
- Take mini-breaks. There will be times when you're feeling drained, but you can't leave the situation for an extended alone time. Maybe you're at a busy work convention, you're on a getaway with friends, or you're visiting family for the holidays. In these circumstances, try to find time to slip away to a quiet corner when it wouldn't be seen as rude. Even 10 or 15 minutes here and there can make a big difference.
- Talk to your family and friends about your alone-time needs. Be upfront about the fact that socializing drains you. It's nothing to be ashamed about and trying to hide it will only add to your social exhaustion. Good friends will be sympathetic and willing to accommodate your needs.

Dealing with social setbacks and rejection

As you put yourself out there socially, there will be times when you feel judged or rejected. Maybe you reached out to someone, but they didn't seem interested in having a conversation or starting a friendship.

There's no question: rejection feels bad. But it's important to remember that it's part of life. Not everyone you approach will be receptive to starting a conversation, let alone becoming friends. Just like dating, meeting new people inevitably comes with some element of rejection. The following tips will help you have an easier time with social setbacks:

- Try not to take things too personally. The other person may be having a bad day, be distracted by other problems, or just not be in a talkative mood. Always remember that rejection has just as much to do with the other person as it does with you.

- Keep things in perspective. Someone else's opinion doesn't define you, and it doesn't mean that no one else will be interested in being your friend. Learn from the experience and try again.

- Don't dwell on mistakes. Even if you said something you regret, for example, it's unlikely that the other person will remember it after a short time. Stay positive; refrain from labeling yourself a failure, or from telling yourself that you'll never be able to make friends. The very shyest people do, and so will you.

Show Off Your Social Self

Yes, its time to show off your social self. So, set your shyness aside and let your social self shine through.

Although, we fear other people virtually as much as we fear spiders and snakes. Studies of anxiety disorders show that social phobia afflicts 55% percent of the world's population, right behind the fear of specific objects and situations. Short of having an officially diagnosable social phobia, though, occasional bouts of shyness can affect everyone. Without warning, you find yourself tongue-tied, afraid of making a public mistake or overwhelmed at the prospect of meeting new people. As a result, your stellar qualities are temporarily sent into hiding by your feelings of awkwardness and embarrassment.

The core of social phobia is the fear of embarrassment. People with this disorder have difficulty performing ordinary tasks in front of other people for fear of making a mistake or doing something that others perceive as foolish. Although you may think of social phobia like fear of public speaking, the actual disorder encompasses a much wider range of circumstances. In extreme forms, socially phobic avoid eating or drinking in public places. They don't want to be seen chewing, swallowing, or far worse, spilling food or liquids.

Although diagnosable conditions of social phobia involve complex disturbances in thoughts, emotions, and perhaps underlying physiology, ordinary shyness can range from occasional bouts of self-consciousness to a broader range of personality traits. When those bouts of self-consciousness strike you, there can be many possible causes.

One reason we fail to shine in a social situation is common egocentrism, the belief that other people are focused entirely on you and, hence, seeing your mistakes. The less confident you are about your abilities, the more likely it is we fear that the eyes on you will be critical. Simple conditioning can also make you hyper-sensitive. If an older relative or teacher constantly harped at you about your posture, for example, you may feel awkward about the way you walk now. Rather than put yourself out there in the bright light of the public eye, you go out of your way to avoid attention. You'll take the back stairs instead of striding through the center of the room to get from one end of a building to the other. If there's no other route available, you'll cling to the outer walls, hoping to melt into the shadows.

As difficult as physical shyness can be, verbal shyness can be even more disabling. It's hard to avoid attention in clutch situations in life in which you are expected to speak, such as a job or school admissions interview. A question is asked, and you are expected to answer. One-on-one social situations can also call for you to step out of your comfort zone. We've all had the stressful moments when we're sitting next to a virtual stranger at a meal or in a party and are expected to keep the conversational ball rolling. The classic scenario of meeting your loved one's friends or relatives for the first time can put anyone on edge, even the best talker in the world. Throw in a touch of shyness, and your anxiety can rapidly escalate.

Progress in the treatment of diagnosable social phobia is coming from the evidence-based treatments using cognitive-behavioral approaches. For example, a therapist can ask their clients to do "homework" in which they analyze the situations that cause them to be most fearful. Armed with the data, the therapists then work with the client to identify the so-called dysfunctional thoughts that crowd their mind and cause their inner panic to skyrocket. Once those thoughts are brought to the surface, the therapist works with the client to challenge and ultimately change them. One of the most critical steps in treating social phobia is overcoming the individual's social isolation. The new thoughts must be practiced in real-life settings for the treatment to work. Starting with small steps, the client can gradually experiment with the new thinking patterns, and feel better in a greater variety of previously threatening situations. Clients can also benefit from relaxation methods, mindfulness, and meditation in coping with the previously crippling feelings of social anxiety.

The same principles can be applied to helping people manage shyness, whether chronic or occasional. Unlike social phobia, ordinary shyness isn't a disabling condition, but it can be problematic when you need to make a favorable impression by what you say or do.

The first step to help you show off your social self is to identify the situations in which your shyness reaches this problematic level and has actually prevented you from reaching the desired goal in life. We learn many of our dysfunctional social behaviors through old-fashioned classical conditioning. Just as you had to deal with the relative criticizing your posture, you may have to lurk in your memory a time when you blurted out a wrong answer to a question that cost you a desirable outcome. Having burned your chances by speaking too quickly, you naturally adapt by taking your time before you answer, or perhaps by saying nothing at all.

Even if you can't remember an exact moment in time when your shyness first took hold, you can nevertheless examine the thoughts going through your head when you've recently felt particularly shy. The chances are good that you felt unduly conscious of making a mistake of some kind or perhaps felt that you were being judged.

Now let's take those thoughts and challenge them. Are you actually being judged as harshly as you think you are? Did you really say or do something worthy of someone's eternal and scathing criticism? Or did you exaggerate its importance in your own mind? Even if the worst case scenario were true, and you did, in fact, offend someone else or say something that made you look bad, are you certain that it bothered the other person as much as it does you? Isn't it possible that the other person actually is willing to forgive you? If someone offended you and then apologized, wouldn't you be willing to consider accepting the apology? How about if someone else tripped in front of you, much to that person's dread? Would you really and truly judge that person as hopelessly clumsy for now and forever more?

You might well argue that this line of questioning is fine if someone already knows you, but what about the impression you make when you meet someone for the first time. Of course, first impressions are important. However, even if you mess up in your first moment of meeting someone by saying or doing something awkwardly, all is not lost. If we go with the "most people are forgiving" theory, it's even possible to make up for that glitch in the situation within milliseconds of its occurrence.

Now turn to the awkward pause in the conversation when you feel that the onus is on you to keep things going. Conversations are two-way streets, so if there's a lull, isn't it up to you to fill it? It's true, that person may be waiting for you to say something, or it might be expected that you do (as in an interview). In those particular situations, though, your job becomes slightly different. Turn down your internal monologue about how badly you're doing and instead focus on what is actually happening in the room. Don't listen to yourself, listen to the other person. Really pay attention to what he or she is asking, not on how miserable you're feeling or what you should say next. You got to that interview for a reason: you look good on paper, you had impressive recommendations, and you are the kind of person that they're looking for. This should help you build your confidence so that you stop worrying about how inadequate you must seem and instead be that person they expected to meet. Your social self will shine even in the toughest interview if you turn down that critical inner voice.

It's also important to recognize the benefits of shyness. Shy people may think that they're flawed when they compare themselves to their extraverted friends and family. However, think of your shyness as an asset. It takes a mix of personalities to make up a well-functioning social environment, whether it's a two-person couple, a large family, a classroom, or a work setting. Too many extroverts in a situation can lead to chaos. They clamor for attention and drown each other out. When something goes wrong, they let you know. You don't have to feel bad or ashamed of yourself just because you're not the noisiest person in the room. Shy people have the virtue of not being the squeaky wheel. Other people will appreciate you for who you are, not how loudly or frequently you make your presence known.

When it comes right down to it, challenging this negative view of yourself may ultimately be the most important step you can take to conquer your bouts with shyness. Accepting your personal qualities will help you focus more on enjoying social situations doing well in them, and giving yourself the confidence to do even better the next time you're in the spotlight.

Improve Your Conversations

HAVE YOU ever thought that some people are just natural conversationalists? No matter whom they're talking to, no matter the topic, they seem relaxed and comfortable. So you start to envy their skills— You want people to listen to you and ask you questions. All these are possible if you do all the things I'm going to talk about in this section. It will take some time, but gradually you will get to learn several different techniques for making a conversation more interesting.

The art of conversation, like any art, is a skill of elegance, nuance and creative execution.

I happen to believe that there is an art to everything we do and why not? Without flair and panache, most things become drudgery. Why settle for drudgery when you can have art?

When it comes to the art of conversation we've all met people who seem to have the knack for it. They can talk to anybody about anything and they seem to do it with complete ease. And while it's true that there are those who are born with the gift of gab, luckily for the rest of us, conversation skills can be developed and mastered.

In the previous chapter of this ebook, I gave some tips for starting a conversation - some easy ways to engage in conversation with someone new. Many of the same tips hold true for developing good conversational skills. Although I didn't really talk much about improving your conversation because we focused on Shyness. But in this section, I'll be going in depth. We'll be focusing on improving our conversation.

What Is Conversation?

A conversation is a form of communication; however, it is usually more spontaneous and less formal. We enter conversations for purposes of pleasant engagement in order to meet new people, to find out information and to enjoy social interactions.

While there is more to having good conversation skills than being a comedian, dramatic actor, or a great storyteller, it is not necessary to become more gregarious, animated, or outgoing. Instead, you can develop the ability to listen attentively, ask fitting questions, and pay attention to the answers - all qualities essential to the art of conversation. With diligent practice and several good pointers, anyone can improve their conversation skills.

Tips on How to Improve Your Conversation

1) Be a good listener. To some people, listening means planning what they are going to say when the other person stops talking. Real listening means focusing on what the other person is saying. One way to stay engaged is to respond to what they're saying: "What you've just said is interesting. Please tell me more about that." Or "Excuse me. Can you explain that again? I didn't quite get it."

Getting to know a new colleague, client, mentor, etc. can often be awkward if you're not confident in your conversation skills.

Luckily, you can practice those skills to be a better

conversationalist, and one of the best ways to do that is through active listening.

- specifically say "active" listening here because it does require action to listen to someone in a way that allows you to respond thoughtfully. The most productive and meaningful conversations happen when both parties are aware of how to listen well.

Here are 8 steps to improve your conversation skills through active listening:

Step 1. Stop what you are doing

If you're going to engage in a conversation with someone, let them know you're listening intently by stopping what you're working on to give them your attention. If someone comes over to you and you don't make eye contact, continue working, and ask what they want, it'll be pretty clear you're not actually ready to listen.

Step 2. Shift your attention

When you're in the middle of something and someone comes over to talk to you, there are a few ways you can respond.

- Jot down a quick note as a reminder of where you left off, then shift your attention to the other person.
- Ask them for a minute to finish writing a sentence or save a document and then turn to them to talk.
- If you're pressed for time at the moment, ask if this is a quick conversation or if you can schedule a time later to talk.

It's okay to let someone know that you're not available to talk right that second. Letting yourself finish a thought or scheduling a better time to talk will allow you to be more focused on the conversation, rather than continuing to think about what you were just doing or need to get done.

Step 3. Clear your mind

While you're shifting gears mentally to start a conversation, try to intentionally clear your mind. It's easy to let your mind wander to what you have to do next, or what's for dinner, or that great story you want to tell a friend, but right now it's time for the conversation at hand. Push those distracting thoughts aside and help yourself focus with the next step…

Step 4. Focus on the other person

Mentally focusing on someone's words is much easier when you are physically focused also. Turn away from your computer, face the person and make eye contact instead of constantly looking around the room. Giving them positive nonverbal signals that you're paying attention helps them to know that you're focused on the conversation.

Step 5. Listen

Alright, the time has come – time to listen.

Now that you're focused on the conversation, you need to maintain focus by actively listening to the other person. People speak at about 150 words per minute, but it's estimated that we think about 400-500 words per minute! That's a lot of extra space between their words and your thoughts to distract you. The next three steps are where you'll keep that space filled with thoughts relevant to the conversation rather than distractions.

Step 6. Write it down

If you hear something important or insightful that you don't want to forget, write it down! If you don't have a pen and paper and want to use your phone, just make sure to let the other person know you're making a note of something they said so they don't think you're ignoring them.

Step 7. Confirm what you heard

Sometimes what someone says doesn't come across the way they're thinking about it. If you're not sure you understand what they're saying (or even if you do), wait until they're done with a thought and then confirm what you took away from what they said.

This is one of those often skipped but highly important conversation skills since it helps the other person be more clear about their thoughts and prevents miscommunication.

Step 8. Process

There is more to Listening than just hearing.

Once you've gone through these steps to ensure you're truly listening to what someone has to say, you can process through it and formulate a response. One of the toughest aspects of listening well is not taking so much thought to respond that you miss what they're actually saying, but still have adequate time to think through what to say.

If you need more time to process, it's okay to tell them! Just make sure to confirm what they were trying to say, and let them know you'll think through it and respond soon.

Also, keep in mind that not every conversation needs a response to fix a problem. Sometimes a person just needs a listening ear but isn't looking for advice. If you're not sure whether to share your advice or not, again – ask!

2) Ensure there is a balance of giving and taking.

A conversation can get boring quickly if one person is doing all the talking while the other is trying to get a word in edgewise. When that happens whoever is not talking begins to tune out and there is no conversation!

There can be many reasons for a lack of giving and taking. Sometimes nervousness can get in the way and you ramble on without realizing it. Or, nervousness can make you freeze and you don't know what to say next. If you find yourself freezing up, take a deep breath and do your best to focus; smile, and then reflect on what you want to say. If the other person is the rambler and you've tried several times to interject but haven't been able to, then excuse yourself politely and move on.

If later on, you realize that you were the rambler, then at least you will have made the most important step towards improvement which is - awareness.

What you have to do is – Determine whether your tendency to dominate a conversation is due to nervousness or self-involvement.

Either way, review the conversation in your head. Look for spots where you could have paused and allowed the other person to talk. For future conversations, a good rule of thumb is after you make a point, pause for either agreement or an alternative point of view. Observe body language for cues whether to stop or continue. For example, is the person glossy-eyed and therefore bored? Are they moving towards you to speak and you just keep on talking? Are they looking elsewhere (for an escape) while you are carrying on? In a good conversation, each person needs to express themselves or it is no longer a conversation but a monologue.

3) Be interesting and have something to say. While you don't have to be a comedian, entertainer, or brilliant raconteur, you do need to be interesting otherwise what would you say? If you are not well informed, tend not to read much, or have very few interests, you will have very little to talk about except yourself. Unfortunately, no one wants to hear about your latest troubles, conquests, or daily routine. Yet so many dull conversationalists believe that's what people want to hear from them. Who hasn't been stuck with someone at a social event who blathers on about their family history, latest job interview, or the like?

To avoid being that person, become knowledgeable about world events, people in the news, or what's going on locally. Take time to keep up with the latest music, new technological discoveries, or recent best sellers. No one can know everything, so if you can enlighten someone during the course of a conversation, you'll be a hit! By the same token, you can learn something new as well.

Of course, not all conversations are knowledge sharing

gatherings or discussions of global import. Many, especially at social functions, consist of light-hearted and cheerful banter. In such cases, be aware of the tone and mood of the conversation and go with the flow. If you are not particularly good at one-liners, or much of a jokester, you can always listen, smile and enjoy the humor. Never act as you feel out of place or ill at ease.

4) Be relaxed, be yourself. If you are on edge or trying to be someone you're not, it will show and therefore doom a conversation to failure before it starts. Admittedly, if you are not relaxed it's hard to appear as if you are. Slow down and take a deep breath. If you don't do your best to relax, you will end up saying something silly, unintelligible, or unrelated to the conversation. Also, smile warmly; it will make you appear pleasant and therefore, more approachable.

Note: if you are trying too hard to be something you're not, you will come across as a fake or a wannabe.

To start a conversation, go up to someone and introduce yourself.

It is both polite and necessary to start things off smoothly. If the occasion calls for it, you can offer a handshake and then smile and make eye contact. Being friendly puts the other person at ease and opens the door for them to introduce themselves. If, for whatever reason, your attempt is not well-received and you notice the other person is cool or standoffish, bow out gracefully and move on. Do not take it as a rejection; merely consider that the person has their reasons for not reciprocating. Perhaps they are not feeling well, have had a bad day, or are not in the mood for conversation.

5) Use the best words. The ability to talk smoothly has a lot to do with choosing the precise words to convey your precise feelings or thoughts. Constantly develop your vocabulary and practice communicating as accurately as possible. It will help you develop a way with words and allow you to express yourself more easily.

6) To improve. Practice and then practice some more. The art of conversation, like any skill, takes practice. Do not expect to be adept after your first few attempts. It will take practice as well as exposure to many different social situations. A good way to get practice before you venture out to an event is with family members and people you are comfortable with. They can give you helpful and supportive feedback, which in turn, gives you something to work on. You can never have too much practice!

Quick-Tips for The Art of Conversation

- Do not dominate a conversation or make it all about you. A monologue is not conversation.
- Show interest and curiosity in others.
- Strive for a balance of giving and taking.
- Be a good listener by maintaining good eye contact and asking pertinent questions.
- Train yourself to relax by using visualization, meditation, or other relaxation methods. Being relaxed is vital for good conversation.
- Do not interrupt and cut in with your own ideas

before the other person is finished speaking.

- Maintain an open mind; everyone has a right to express themselves even if you don't agree with what they are saying.
- Although this is cliché, try to avoid topics such as sex, religion, and politics. You would be surprised at how many people get trapped by them and end up in verbal battle, not conversation.
- Be prepared by staying on top of the latest news, developments and world events.
- Be approachable by staying relaxed, smiling and maintaining a friendly attitude.

Possessing the art of conversation do not just improve your social skills, but also personal and work relationships. It gives you the opportunity to meet interesting new people and introduces you to various new topics and subject matter. With practice and application, anyone can improve their conversation skills.

Using Effective Conversation Skills to Influence Key Business Partners and Peers

Effective conversation skills are essential for achieving success. Beginning with active listening and continuing with clear correspondence, this strategy can maintain the respect necessary to influence your business partners and peers. It holds the power to motivate, stimulate creativity, and promote competitiveness to produce the best outcomes. The most successful people use a conversational style that is proactive, allowing them to work closely with others within their network and negotiate to achieve mutually beneficial goals.

Active listening allows multiple perspectives to be understood and creates a well-rounded view of the goals as well as the steps necessary to achieve them. Do not simply wait to speak. It's important to filter out the noise, read between the lines, and decipher what is truly important. Having an inquisitive nature and being willing to learn ensures that everyone is moving in the proper direction together.

To further ensure business partners and peers are on the same page, the conversation must continue in a thorough and efficient manner. This means being clear and concise while being assertive and confidently addressing all aspects of the discussion. Always say what you mean and mean what you say. When a potential roadblock is identified, courteously confront issues directly. By solving problems quickly, it is possible to produce immediate results with lasting positive outcomes.

Especially for internal conversation, honesty and realism can be key influencers. By maintaining a detailed, realistic understanding of the current situation, expectations of what needs to be completed, trust and confidence will be reinforced. Expressing the "why" and "how" (including measurable performance indicators) can help to motivate business partners and peers by illustrating success within reach.

It is critical to ask "why" and "how" when obtaining information in addition to facilitating it. Questions are the backbone of effective conversation because they offer clarity. Take ownership of your work and limitations –

know when to ask for additional resources. There is no better way to get information from peers than to ask them for assistance.

While interacting with many people within a business setting, interpreting individual personality traits and approaching those people differently ensures effective conversation on a 1-to-1 level. For example, it is often necessary to actively open lines of conversation with people who don't speak up on their own. Some people respond better in an individual setting as opposed to a group. In any case, being respectful of everyone's time, energy, knowledge, and authority facilitate collaboration.

Even when faced with challenging situations, remaining level-headed and positive upholds high morale. Constructive criticism must embrace strengths to set others on a path to success. There are likely many ways to accomplish overarching goals and even more opinions about what is best. An effective team shares its knowledge and empowers each other to learn and understand new approaches. A mutually beneficial result can be reached while staying true to the strategic initiatives of each business partner and peer. Often, leveraging the team's existing strengths presents an opportunity to advocate for change and excel in a new realm.

From the subject matter to the audience receiving the information, a thorough understanding is necessary to communicate effectively. Strong interdepartmental collaboration and information delivery can help obtain success in all business aspects.

Why Having a Good Conversation Skill Is Important

For Instance; In your career, You may have all the necessary technical skills, the expertise and the experience that can really attest that you deserve that next promotion, but if you haven't got the conversation skills to back it up, you might miss the opportunity to level up in your career.

It is important to be able to have the conversation skills to communicate everything that will contribute for your career growth. You can't just silently plug away at your work without being open to opportunities for growth. You can actually make changes by means of using your conversation skills.

Conversation skills are important to any kinds of career because it is the base means with which you express yourself to other people, specifically your colleagues, your boss and other people you will deal with in the career you have chosen for yourself. Many competent graduates have missed out on opportunities for a rewarding career because they lacked the ample amount of conversation skills needed to be able to sustain the communication dynamics that come with every sort of promotion in work.

From the very beginning of your career, conversation skills are some sort of gauge with which other people measure your capability, coupled with your array of experiences and qualifications shown over a steady stream of performance for a set period of time. Conversation skills in itself will not land you the promotion or career growth you aspire, but a lack of it will certainly lessen your likelihood of bagging a good job, especially if they have seen better conversationalists among your colleagues who may be aspiring for the same career growth form that you want.

Having good conversation skills does not only give a good edge compared to your colleagues, but it will also help you gain the general goodwill of most people in your workplace. If you are as gracious with your words as you are excellent with your work, people will just naturally trust you and establish you as someone who is reliable and fun to work with. Good conversation skills ease the gaps that come between people who have little or almost nothing in common.

Not all career growth opportunities are easily bestowed. You might find your efforts less visible to the people who can help you land that promotion. In this case, you will definitely need to be backed up by your subtle and well-thought out conversation skill strategies that will help you be able to express yourself and assert your qualification to your bosses without making them feel threatened or imposed upon.

Conversation skills do not only deal with the fluent pronunciation, the good articulation or the well-versed array of words. Veering from the technical aspect is the emotional correspondence which makes your eloquent speaking capabilities more felt by those who will hear you and converse with you. Body language is also a great factor which will either make or break your statements (We'll also be looking at Body Language in this book). A good investment as you grow in your career is to enhance or refresh your conversation skills. All the information put together in this section is what you need to Improve, as well as enhance and refresh your conversation skill.

If you are a person with good conversation skills, you also naturally inspire others to do the same thing even without trying. Good conversation skills are not just admirable, it is also contagious especially with people you interact with on a regular basis. If you are a catalyst to having good conversation skills at work, you can also expect your colleagues and consequently, your entire company, to grow well with you in that arena. Having good conversation skills is like shining a flashlight on what is otherwise considered as a typical work routine day. In addition to that, if you have cultivated yourself to attain good conversation skills, you will definitely reap what you sow by means of meeting more interesting people who can match your conversation skills and double your growth, professionally as well as personally.

Build Genuine Relationships

This is a one size fits all guide to building the right kind of relationship.

How many of us have learned how to build genuine relationships? Where did we learn? At home? At school? There are art and science to building genuine relationships.

In this section, I want to give you some practical tips on how you can build genuine relationships — the kinds of relationships that cannot be scaled.

7 Tips for Building Genuine Relationships

Here are 7 tips on how you can build genuine, sincere relationships:

1. Create a safe environment where you can trust and share openly without fear.

Don't interrupt, even if you need to put your hand over your mouth to stop yourself. Learn to fight fairly. No name calling. Don't make threats. Apologize when you know you should. If you're too angry to really listen, stop! Go into another room, take space for yourself, breathe, and calm down.

2. Talk to Everyone.

A great way to build genuine relationships is by making an effort to talk to as many people as you can.

Making an effort to talk to more random strangers will actually bring you more feelings of happiness, in spite of widespread notions that you would be happier keeping to yourselves. Similarly, making an effort to talk to more people can also help you to build more genuine relationships.

- simple "Hello" or "How are you?" may be all it takes to get a conversation started, and then you are off to the races. You never know who you might be in line with at the grocery store or at a department store, especially during the holidays, when more people venture out of their homes. You can strike up a conversation and create a brand new relationship.

3. Separate the facts from the feelings.

What beliefs and feelings get triggered in you during conflicts? Ask yourself: Is there something from my past that is influencing how I'm seeing the situation now? The critical questions you want to ask: Is this about him or her, or is it really about me? What's the real truth?

Once you're able to differentiate facts from feelings, you'll see your partner more clearly and be able to resolve conflicts from clarity.

4. Develop compassion.

Practice observing yourself and your partner without judging. Part of you might judge, but you don't have to identify with it. Judging closes a door. The opposite of judging is compassion. When you are compassionate, you are open, connected, and more available to dialoguing respectfully with your partner. As you increasingly learn to see your partner compassionately, you will have more power to choose your response rather than just reacting.

5. Make time for your relationship.

No matter who you are or what your work is, you need to nurture your relationship. Make sure you schedule time for the well-being of your relationship. That includes "hanging out" and also taking downtime together. Frequently create a sacred space together by shutting off all things technological and digital. Like a garden, the more you tend to your relationship, the more it will grow.

- **Take Extraordinary Measures to Delight the People You Meet**

You should learn to take extraordinary measures not just to acquire users, but also to make them happy. This advice can apply not just to start-up businesses, but to the people you come across as well — you should take extraordinary measures to not just acquire friends, but also to make them happy.

As an example, a company that helps people to build online forms. When it was just starting out, someone at the company just sends each new user a hand-written thank you note. Can you imagine the impression that made on their early adopters?

What if we all took this approach to life? What if we all tried to delight the people we meet?

You may be chortling under your breath at this suggestion (I can hear you.) But why not? In my experience, it doesn't take much to delight people, because the bar is generally set pretty low. For example, you could dash off a quick, hand-written note to the next person you meet, or maybe to some guy who wrote a super helpful guest post you just read (hint hint). You may just create a friend and an advocate for life.

7. Take a Genuine Interest in Others

At the core of building relationships in a genuine way is taking interest in the people you meet. And taking interest in a person is, by definition, a genuine activity. It requires that you drill down and devote your solitary attention to one person.

If you want to make sure your interests are perceived as genuine, then focus on the following:

- Listen intently and ask good questions. Be completely present with the person, by putting away your phone, making eye contact, listening to what they have to say, and asking good questions. Nothing builds rapport more than being curious about the other person.

- Focus on the details. Remember details about the people you meet, such as their hobbies, their children's names, or their hometown. Don't expect to keep all of these details in your head. Personally, I write them down using my dairy, but you could do it whatever way works for you.

- Remember names. Here's another detail you don't want to forget: the person's name! Remembering people's names is a fast way to build trust.

- Follow up.

    Following up with people demonstrates your interest in them was genuine and sincere, and not limited to when they are in front of you. Follow up by sending the person you've met invitations to special events, by making helpful introductions, or by sharing resources or relevant information. For example, if I had a conversation where I recommended a great coffee company, I might follow up with an email including a link to the coffee company.

How Being an Interesting Person Can Help You Build Genuine Relationships

Are You an Interesting Person?

In our culture today much emphasis is placed on looks, sex appeal and being youthful. Many individuals spend a disproportionate amount of time working on their outer packages.

Rather than being introspective, they go to great lengths to be fashionable and trendy as well as making sure they are seen at the latest "in" places.

Sadly, when little or no effort is being made to develop the intellect or an interesting personality, many good-looking young men and women come across as being flighty and uninformed, as well as self-centered and self-absorbed.

Evidence of this unhealthy trend can be witnessed in the behavior of some of today's young celebrities and pop stars who often serve as role models (whether we like it or not) for our children.

We are bombarded daily with news of their antics where they engage in self-indulgent and often irresponsible behavior. Some of them end up in a rehab which quite often doesn't address the real problem.

Although physical attraction is very helpful in the preservation of our species, evolution has come a long way in giving us more than solely our appearance to attract each other.

For a solid, meaningful relationship to develop between two parties they must have more to contribute to each other beyond their initial physical attraction.

When two people have little in common except for their good looks, there is virtually no place for a relationship to go. Instead, they must enjoy each other as individuals and be able to develop a bond or friendship. There must be substance, shared interests, willingness to grow, and mutual respect.

So, What Is the Answer?

Become someone whose company others seek. Have something meaningful to contribute. Not only will you enrich your own life in the process, but you will also enrich the lives of others. Short and Simple!

Here are some ways you can become an interesting person:

- Cultivate a variety of interests
- Expand your knowledge in the arts, music, literature, sports
- Take a genuine interest in others
- Read more
- Stay on top of current events
- Express your informed opinions
- Become a good conversationalist
- Be aware
- Develop and appreciate humor
- Develop good conversation skills

- Be self-confident

Moreover, developing all aspects of your self - your mind, body, intellect, and spirit. It's never too late to start!

Building Genuine Relationships for Business

Customer relationships are one of the most important parts of your business, if not the most important. So, how do you begin building those Genuine, meaningful, and lifelong relationships with customers?

We are writers, entrepreneurs, bloggers, influencers, people, and humans. At our core, we are people that want others to do business with us, to get our name out there. But from well-established businesses to the small start-up, there is one thing that we need to be doing to truly grow; which is having genuine relationships. To sit down and actually have good conversations with your potential or existing customers.

Customer relationship building starts before someone even makes a purchase. In this section, I have laid out tips that will help you to build Genuine relationships with your clients/customers successfully.

Building a genuine relationship is undoubtedly a struggle for a lot of people for a variety of reasons even outside of work. So it's to be expected businesses to run into the same sort of problems. We are people behind the business at the end of the day.

You can start fixing a lot of those issues by doing the following things listed below:

- Engage with a person, ask questions

As a business person, you should learn to ask your customers/clients questions. Not necessarily about what it is they do because sometimes they seem boring and unnecessary. Instead, ask about why they followed you on social media. What got them to be a consumer of your product or service?

Understanding a person's reasoning can be meaningful once you grow a massive audience. Also questions in general help in getting an idea of the person as well.

Asking questions shows you are interested, that you actually care.

- Ask about passions or hobbies

Yes, it is necessary for you to know about the passions or hobbies of your customers or potential clients. Not necessarily to build up more of a demographic but you can understand what people are passionate about. When you are an author like myself, your brand is you. In my case, I'm the only employee for myself so it's important for me to get along with other people.

- Show your authenticity

Some of these tactics can be difficult if you have more people involved in a business. However, there are more creative ways to show authenticity to others. For someone flying solo, it's a matter of being personal.

I take pride in showing off my changes, what I'm up to, and inspiring people in my own way. Businesses can do the same by showing behind the scenes stuff, asking for suggestions and so on. This helps you build and maintain genuine relationships with your customers.

- Be Responsive and Personal

Timely and efficient communication is absolutely imperative as a business owner. Being available to clients is key to letting them know their business and satisfaction are important to you. Make sure you are responding to their phone calls and emails professionally and in a timely manner.

Although you want to be efficient, making the time to connect with clients is a core element of building genuine relationships with them. Make it a point to get to know them, whether that is asking them about their family vacation they just went on or how their new puppy is doing. Of course, your product or service is always the number one focus, but it is important for you to let your clients know that you acknowledge them and see them as a person, more than solely a business asset.

- Share Knowledge

Chances are your company is filled with a number of amazing services or products. If your client doesn't understand your area of expertise, they may feel intimidated about the intricacies of your business, and therefore disconnected. This is an opportunity to share information.

Helping your client understand what your business is all about will build trust and confidence in the process. Explaining to the client what you do, why you do it, and how you make decisions will help them feel more comfortable with you as a business partner. You can even add in your own story of why you got started in this industry and how you've seen your business grow to give it personal touch.

- Be Open to Feedback

Be grateful for the feedback received from clients; both good and not so good. It may be difficult to hear feedback that you may not have been anticipating. Be open to receiving these comments and see if there are any aspects of your business that could be improved.

There may be an issue in your firm you were blind to before a customer brought it up. Thank them for sharing their thoughts with you and work to solve any problems they are experiencing in a kind, thoughtful way. This will go a long way in building a genuine relationship with that client. This will also help in building trust and credibility with your clients.

- Set Realistic Expectations

Consider the famous quote, "Under-promise and over-deliver." This is essential to remember when working with clients. Overestimate deadlines so that when your team finishes a project before the deadline, your client will be nothing short of thrilled. One of the most detrimental things to your relationship with a client is to overcommit and under-deliver.

Building trust in an untrusting world is essential. Once your clients trust you, they become loyal to you. And, loyal customers are your best referrals!

Get Started Building Your Genuine Relationships

Now it's time for you to get started. Take the advice above

and begin building genuine relationships, whether at work, school, or home, etc. Don't worry if your system is not perfect. Don't think about optimization or making sure you are maximizing your efficiency.

It doesn't matter so much where you begin or where you end up, but just that you get started. You have to start somewhere. Just take it one relationship at a time.

Body Language

What Is Body Language?

Body language is a non-verbal form of communication using physical movements and behaviors rather than words. The expressions and postures used in body language can be used to understand how others feel about a situation and the people involved. Facial expressions and posture are both considered body language, recognizing these expressions and postures as a cue to how someone feels can change the whole dynamic of a situation.

When someone smiles, everyone recognizes it as a welcoming, happy expression, but what if that person smiles to be polite but they are not happy about the situation? Reading body language involves more than an obvious facial expression, how that person is standing about others in the conversation, their posture, and their eyes can tell you more about that smile.

Many body language cues are not conscious, slight changes in facial expressions and posture can be telling about how someone feels, and they may not even realize they are giving away their thoughts. The tone of someone's voice and involuntary muscle movements are also considered body language; detectives even use knowledge of these involuntary language cues to help them read situations and people during investigations.

Relationships are built on communication. I share with you, and you share with me. When we share with each other, we understand each other better, which grows our relationship deeper.

The tricky part is that a lot of conversation is non-verbal. I might not use words to tell you if I feel upset with you, but

I will physically draw back from you---for instance, by crossing my arms, angling my feet towards the door, or avoiding eye contact. If you don't catch my physical signals, you might not realize that something is wrong until it's too late.

Even if you understand the body language signals other people are sending, you might not realize what your own body is communicating. When your body language is cold and standoffish, people are unlikely to approach you, even if you want them to.

Fortunately, it's easy to make body language a positive part of your interactions. In this section, I will walk you through the simple, practical principles that will guide you to a great interpretation of body language and how you can improve your Social skills with them.

Here's what to look for when you're trying to interpret body language.

- Facial Expressions

Think for a moment about how much a person is able to convey with just a facial expression. A smile can indicate approval or happiness. A frown can signal disapproval or unhappiness. In some cases, our facial expressions may reveal our true feelings about a particular situation. While you say that you are feeling fine, the look on your face may tell people otherwise.

Just a few examples of emotions that can be expressed via facial expressions include:

- Happiness
- Sadness
- Anger
- Surprise
- Disgust
- Fear
- Confusion
- Excitement
- Desire
- Contempt

The expression on a person's face can even help determine if we trust or believe what the individual is saying. One study found that the most trustworthy facial expression involved a slight raise of the eyebrows and a slight smile. This expression, the researchers suggested, conveys both friendliness and confidence.

Facial expressions are also among the most universal forms of body language. The expressions used to convey fear, anger, sadness, and happiness are similar throughout the world.

Research even suggests that we make judgments about people's intelligence based on their faces and expressions. One study found that individuals who had narrower faces and more prominent noses were more likely to be perceived as intelligent. People with smiling, joyful expression were also judged as being more intelligent than those with angry expressions.

- The Eyes

The eyes are frequently referred to as the "windows to the soul" since they are capable of revealing a great deal about what a person is feeling or thinking. As you engage in conversation with another person, taking note of eye movements is a natural and important part of the communication process. Some common things you may notice include whether people are making direct eye contact or averting their gaze, how much they are blinking, or if their pupils are dilated.

When evaluating body language, pay attention to the following eye signals:

Eye gaze: When a person looks directly into your eyes while having a conversation, it indicates that they are interested in and paying attention. However, prolonged eye contact can feel threatening. On the other hand, breaking eye contact and frequently looking away might indicate that the person is distracted, uncomfortable, or trying to conceal his or her real feelings.

Blinking: Blinking is natural, but you should also pay attention to whether a person is blinking too much or too little. People often blink more rapidly when they are feeling distressed or uncomfortable. Infrequent blinking may indicate that a person is intentionally trying to control his or her eye movements. For example, a poker player might blink less frequently because he is purposely trying to appear unexcited about the hand he was dealt with.

Pupil size: Pupil size can be a very subtle nonverbal communication signal. While light levels in the environment control pupil dilation, sometimes emotions can also cause small changes in pupil size. For example, you may have heard the phrase "bedroom eyes" used to describe the look someone gives when they are attracted to another person. Highly dilated eyes, for example, can indicate that a person is interested or even aroused.

- The Mouth

Mouth expressions and movements can also be essential in reading body language. For example, chewing on the bottom lip may indicate that the individual is experiencing feelings of worry, fear, or insecurity.

Covering the mouth may be an effort to be polite if the person is yawning or coughing, but it may also be an attempt to cover up a frown of disapproval. Smiling is perhaps one of the greatest body language signals, but smiles can also be interpreted in many ways. A smile may be genuine, or it may be used to express false happiness, sarcasm, or even cynicism.

When evaluating body language, pay attention to the following mouth and lip signals:

Pursed lips: Tightening the lips might be an indicator of distaste, disapproval, or distrust.

Lip biting: People sometimes bite their lips when they are worried, anxious, or stressed.

Covering the mouth: When people want to hide an emotional reaction, they might cover their mouths in order to avoid displaying smiles or smirks.

Turned up or down: Slight changes in the mouth can also be subtle indicators of what a person is feeling. When the mouth is slightly turned up, it might mean that the person is feeling happy or optimistic. On the other hand, a slightly down-turned mouth can be an indicator of sadness, disapproval, or even an outright grimace.

- The Arms and Legs

The arms and legs can also be useful in conveying nonverbal information. Crossing the arms can indicate defensiveness. Crossing legs away from another person may indicate dislike or discomfort with that individual.

Other subtle signals such as expanding the arms widely may be an attempt to seem larger or more commanding while keeping the arms close to the body may be an effort to minimize oneself or withdraw from attention.

When you are evaluating body language, pay attention to some of the following signals that the arms and legs may convey:

- Crossed arms might indicate that a person feels defensive, self-protective, or closed-off.
- Standing with hands placed on the hips can be an indication that a person is ready and in control, or it can also possibly be a sign of aggressiveness.
- Clasping the hands behind the back might indicate that a person is feeling bored, anxious, or even

angry.

- Rapidly tapping fingers or fidgeting can be a sign that a person is bored, impatient, or frustrated.
- Crossed legs can indicate that a person is feeling closed off or in need of privacy.

- Posture

How we hold our bodies can also serve as an important part of body language. The term posture refers to how we hold our bodies as well as the overall physical form of an individual. Posture can convey a wealth of information about how a person is feeling as well as hints about personality characteristics, such as whether a person is confident, open, or submissive.

Sitting up straight, for example, may indicate that a person is focused and paying attention to what's going on. Sitting with the body hunched forward, on the other hand, can imply that the person is bored or indifferent.

When you are trying to read body language, try to notice some of the signals that a person's posture can send.

- Open posture involves keeping the trunk of the body open and exposed. This type of posture indicates friendliness, openness, and willingness.
- Closed posture involves hiding the trunk of the body often by hunching forward and keeping the arms and legs crossed. This type of posture can be an indicator of hostility, unfriendliness, and anxiety.

Now you know how to interpret body language, let's look at how you can improve your Social skills with the body language tips below.

Improve Your Social Skills with These 10 Body Language Tips

For every occasion, there's always this one individual who seems to captivate everyone. Her smile lights up the room, people gather to talk to her, and you can't help but be drawn to her. She may not be the prettiest person at the event, but something about her feels exciting and inviting.

Who is she? How is she able to appear so likable to both men and women?

The answer is not in her choice of clothing or her witty remarks (although those are important, too). Her allure comes from her body language. Want to capture the audience the next time you walk into a party? Practice these 10 tips and you'll be on your way to improving your Social skills.

1. Have an open and relaxed posture.

Whether you're standing, sitting, or walking, having the right posture not only makes you look charming, it also helps you to appear taller. If you've been slouching for a long time, there are plenty of easy exercises to fix your stance. It also helps to observe yourself using a full-length mirror. Sit, walk, and stand in front of it for about 5-10 minutes each day until you have the correct posture. This means:

- Head straight and relaxed

- Shoulders back
- Abdomen in
- Knees slightly bent

Once you have mastered good posture, you'll find that you feel more comfortable and confident when facing people.

2. Smile with your eyes.

Your smile is one of your most potent weapons to make you likable instantly. A genuine smile is supposed to reach your eyes, creating tiny crinkles that light up your face. This suggests that you are truly happy, and nothing is more attractive than a person who smiles as they mean it. According to research, smiling also alleviates stress and can influence your level of success.

Believe it or not, you can enhance your smile simply by practicing it every day! Face a mirror, take a deep breath, hold it, and slowly exhale before smiling. You'll notice that you feel more relaxed and your smile looks genuine. Try this a couple more times until you feel confident!

3. Subtly mirror tiny movements.

Mirroring is a body language technique that successful people use to gain rapport. When done right, it should make you more likable without much effort. It's part of our psychology to respond positively to individuals who are like us. In fact, a baby's body functions (like its heartbeat) sync with the mother even before birth.

Good mirroring begins by first observing the other person's movements. Is he leaning forward? Crossing his legs? Nodding? Reflect these actions with your own body to quickly develop a bond of trust. This method has been proven numerous times in different experiments. So at your next party, watch people closely. Mirror their movements to connect better with any person in the room.

4. Use a quick touch on the forearm or shoulder.

Don't underestimate the power of a quick pat on the back or a friendly touch on the arm. Unlike words, these are universally understood and can convey more meaning. For example, if you really like a person, you may lightly touch their arm during a conversation. Similar to mirroring, this builds rapport with the people you meet. Remember not to overdo this though! Just a light tap is enough — never linger!

5. Maintain good eye contact.

There's no doubt that making eye contact is one of the most powerful body language arsenals. However, doing it wrong will make you look creepy. Combine this with tip #2: smile while making eye contact to make yourself irresistible instantly. Ten seconds is a safe time limit before looking elsewhere. Otherwise, you will trigger a person's defense mechanism and make them feel uncomfortable.

6. Turn your body towards the person.

Also known as the "big baby pivot," this involves turning your entire body towards another person. This body language trick got its name from the way most folks turn their attention to a baby. When being introduced to someone, make sure to give your undivided attention by pivoting your body towards them. This delivers the message that they're special and you're interested in them. True interest in another person makes you super sociable in return!

7. Use open hand gestures.

The handshake that we practice today is, in fact, an early custom to prove that you're not hiding any weapons. That's why we have suspicions when people don't show their hands. With this in mind, use gestures to make you the most Sociable person in the room.

When conversing or speaking to a crowd, use certain hand gestures to create an impact. Here are a few:

- Use your fingers when listing points.
- A solid fist means you're determined.
- Make a sweeping motion to mean "everything".
- Bring hands to your chest when talking about a personal experience.

Consider your audience when using hand gestures.

Note: one sign could mean a world of difference in another culture, so use with caution!

8. Pause for a few seconds.

This is a subtle yet very effective part of your body language. You can implement quick pauses during conversations or speeches when:

- You're asked a difficult or personal question (this gives you enough time to think of a good answer).

- You want to build a dramatic effect (pausing between statements is a sign that you're about to deliver big news).

- You want to create an air of mystery (particularly when coupled with a small smile).

- Pausing is also great when used just before you smile. It shows that you're not someone who gives it away so easily.

9. Nod to show confidence in opinion.

According to one study, nodding doesn't necessarily mean that you agree with something. Rather, this simple action strengthens an already existing opinion. In a gathering, for instance, nodding your head to the speaker reinforces whatever he or she is saying. This creates a connection between you two — even if you don't really agree with everything they say. It's also a sign that shows you're paying attention.

10. Avoid fidgeting.

Feeling nervous during an important event? Need to calm your nerves before meeting with clients? If you want to be instantly sociable, one of the things you should avoid is looking restless. If you have the habit of fiddling with your fingers when worried, it could signal to others that you're insecure. Project an appealing aura by standing tall yet relaxed.

If you're still feeling anxious, be sure to bring something familiar with you, like your favorite pen or necklace. These are usually called "comfort objects." According to experts, carrying something you associate with good memories will help reduce anxiety. Look at it or hold it in your hand for a few seconds to remind you that everything's going to be okay. Then, proceed to be your best, irresistible, sociable self!

When Your Body Language and Your Words Don't Agree

Unfortunately, most people don't think about their own body language. They might spend a lot of time thinking of the perfect words to say, but never realize that their body language and their words are sending very different messages.

For example, say you have had a long, hard day, but your friend wants to talk with you about something that they are struggling with. You obviously care about your friend, so you tell them that you want to talk.

But if during the conversation you are yawning, looking at the clock, and leaning back in your chair with your arms crossed, your friend might conclude that you don't really want to talk with them after all. They storm off, and you are left wondering what you said wrong. (Of course, you didn't say anything wrong---that's the point!)

That's just one example; it's easy to think of other ways your own body language can create misunderstandings. When your words and your body are sending different messages, people will tend to go with the message that your body is sending. If you didn't mean to send that message, trouble ensues.

The Power of Self-Awareness

Fortunately, that trouble is entirely avoidable. Just be aware of the messages your body is sending. Your body is going to communicate---that's just part of being human. Take the time to notice what it is communicating, and you can make sure that your body and your words are sending the same message.

Let me be clear. I'm not talking about changing your body language to mask deception---if your words are communicating something untrue, then you should change your words instead of your body language. Relationships built on deception will never give you the long-term satisfaction and intimacy that you need.

Instead, focus on presenting a cohesive, genuine message of the thing that is both true and most important. If you are tired but you care about your friend, the message that is most important is "I care about you" not "I'm tired" (even though both messages are true.) If you are excited to meet someone new but also nervous, the message that is most important is "I am excited to meet you" not "I am nervous."

The message of "I care about you" is more important than the message of "I am very tired", because your commitment to your friend runs deeper than your physical fatigue. The message of "I am excited to meet you" is more important than the message of "I'm feeling nervous" because your desire to make a new friend is greater than your nervousness.

It's okay to make sure your body language communicates the message that is most important. That's not deception; just making sure the most important message is communicated well. When you are aware of your own body language, it allows you to be sure that both your words and your body language reflect the message that is most true.

So take the time to be aware of your own body language. The lists of comfort and discomfort signals are just as useful when you are using them to understand your own body language. Be aware of what your body is communicating, and make the effort to mute discomfort signals and broadcast comfort signals. You'll find that as you match your body language to your words, you will have much greater success in your interactions.

Practicing and Using Body Language to Better Your Social Skills

The best way to practice body language is to mimic the posture, gesture, and facial expression in a full-length mirror. Using a mirror will help you control your body language and use it to express what you want, when you want. This practice technique will help you recognize body language cues from others as well as recognize your postures, gestures and facial expressions.

You can practice micro expressions in a mirror too. If you practice making them enough, you will eventually be able to recognize them in others. You can also look up images of micro-expressions on the internet and use them to help you recognize them.

You will not be able to control micro-expressions, but you can learn to control your posture, gestures and facial expressions. Mastering body language will help you eliminate any unwanted postures, expressions or gestures from ruining your first impression or interfering in social situations. You can use body language to put people at ease during meetings, appear interested and curious when conversations get boring, and generally improve your social interactions in all situations.

Everyone can benefit from learning to read body language. Reading body language can help you save social interactions that are becoming awkward, or boring. This skill can also help you improve your social skills by recognizing body language cues that show someone is ready to leave, in a hurry, un-interested, or intimidated. The more you know, the easier it is to use this skill; eventually it will become second nature and your social skills will improve naturally.

Stop Procrastinating

Why so many people procrastinate and how it can be overcome.

For most people, procrastination, irrespective of what they say, is not about being lazy. In fact, for them, when they procrastinate they often work intensely for long stretches just before their deadlines. Working long and hard is the opposite of lazy, so that can't be the reason we do it. So, why do we procrastinate and, more importantly, what can we do about it?

As suggested above, some say they procrastinate because they are lazy. Others claim they "do better" when they procrastinate. I encourage you to be critical and reflective of these explanations. Virtually everyone who says this habitually procrastinates and has not completed an important academic task or has not reached out to that person they want to be friends with which they planned to.

If you pretty much always procrastinate, and never really approach your wants, then you can't accurately say that you know you do better. Still other people say they like the rush of leaving things to the end and meeting a deadline. But they usually say this when they are NOT working under that deadline. They say this works before or after cramming when they have forgotten the negative consequences of procrastinating such as feelings of anxiety and stress, fatigue, and disappointment from falling below their own standards and having to put their life on hold for chunks of time. Not to mention, leaving things to the end dramatically increases the chances something will go wrong - like getting sick or a computer problem - and you not being able to socialize with people you ought to. So, procrastination can be hard on us and actually increase our chances of failing, but we do it anyway. How come?

Also, when it comes to socializing, procrastination is not a matter, solely, of having poor social skills, either, but rather can be traced to underlying and more complex psychological reasons. For example, if you procrastinate, then you always have the excuse of not going to events you planned to, so your sense of your ability is never threatened.

Procrastination also affects students. For example, In school, when there is so much pressure on getting a good grade on, say, a paper, it's no wonder that students want to avoid it and so put off their work. For the most part, our reasons for delaying and avoiding are rooted in fear and anxiety about doing poorly, of doing too well, of losing control, of looking stupid, of having one's sense of self or self-concept challenged. We avoid doing things to avoid our abilities being judged. And, if we happened to succeed, we feel that much "smarter.". So, what can we do to overcome our tendencies to procrastinate?

Now, before I show you the EXACT steps you can take to demolish procrastination. First, you need to have an understanding of the REASONS WHY you procrastinate and the function procrastination serves in your life. You can't come up with an effective solution if you don't really understand the root of the problem. As with most problems, awareness and self-knowledge are the keys to figuring out how to stop procrastinating. For a lot of people acquiring this insight about how procrastination protects them from feeling like they are not able enough, and keeping it in mind when they are tempted to fall into familiar, unproductive, procrastinating habits goes a long way to solving the problem.

How to stop procrastinating in 5 steps

In this section, I want to show you how to stop procrastinating in 5 simple steps. You need to stop waiting for motivation to strike and take action today.

Step 1: Be brutally honest about your priorities

How often has someone asked you to do something and you told them, "I don't have enough time for that right now."

For example:

FRIEND: Hey, do you want to check out that new bar tonight?

YOU: Sorry, I'm super busy tonight. Maybe some other time. (Proceed to stay at home, binge-watching Netflix all night.)

Another example:

FRIEND: I'm going to take that improv class you said you were interested in. Want to join?

YOU: Ugh sorry, I don't have enough time right now.

We LOVE using "time" as an excuse because it's easy. Who is going to accuse you of having too much time on your hands? Nobody.

When we make this excuse, however, we only cheat ourselves and we kill our social skill.

Instead, it's better to be honest with yourself and others and say, "I appreciate the offer, but that's just not a priority for me right now." Doing this forces you to confront the lies you often tell yourself — and helps you recognize what is important to you ... and what isn't.

Plus, who would you admire more? The person who says, "I don't have enough time" and doesn't show up to anything, or the person who tells you, "I appreciate the offer but that's just not one of my priorities right now?"

Of course, it's the person who is honest with you.

Once you start recognizing what is NOT a priority, you'll start recognizing things that ARE.

ACTION STEP: Be honest and evaluate your priorities.

To help you evaluate what is a priority for you, I highly recommend what I call an "honesty bath."

To do this, keep track of the goals you make for this month. Record them with a Word doc, pen and paper, Excel, whatever. Then put them in a drawer and set a calendar alert for the last day of the month.

At the end of the month, go through the list and see which ones you actually accomplished and which ones you didn't get to. Then decide whether you're going to:

Delete

Defer

Do it

If you say that you're going to say "Hi" to someone in your school, but whenever you see the person coming your way, you just look away and pass ...you're NOT going to talk to that person.

Delete.

If you claim you're going to stay back and attend your youth meeting in church with your fellow youths every Sunday after service, and you haven't done that in a month after saying "You will", guess what? You're NOT going to stay back for that meeting.

Defer.

Are you actually headed to the gym 3x/week with your colleagues like you said you would? Keep DOING IT.

This takes a lot of self-awareness and determination because you have to be ruthlessly honest about your strengths and weaknesses. But by looking at your past behavior, you can drastically change your future behavior for the better.

The best part? It stops that low-level anxiety we all get from having a bunch of goals bouncing around in our head. Once you make the decision, you can live guilt-free and use your energy to commit to things you'll actually do.

Step 2: Stop feeling guilty

It's interesting how people fall into the paradox of guilt — and don't even realize it's happening.

How often have you talked to a friend about working out,

partying, or socializing with people in school, and heard them say something like, "Yeah, I know I really should be doing that but..." followed by some lame excuse as to why they're procrastinating on something important?

"I know I really should be doing that" is just code for "I'm not going to do that at all."

It's the same with people in credit card debt — many don't even know how much debt they have! They'd rather avoid their statements and bury their head in the sand than face the reality of how much they owe.

Why does this happen? Guilt. Plain and simple. It's the reason why we brush things off with meaningless excuses and run away from the actual issue.

If you truly want to stop procrastinating and improve your social skills, as well as become a productivity machine, you need to hold yourself accountable.

ACTION STEP: Don't run away from your guilt.

When you do feel guilty, take these four steps to address it.

1: Acknowledge the guilt.

When you realize that you feel guilty about something you're putting off — like not hitting up the gym or socializing with folks around you — I want you to just take

a moment and acknowledge the feeling. Recognize your guilt and ask yourself what is making you feel guilty. That leads us to...

2: Use the "five whys" technique.

At the heart of this technique is the question "why?" The idea is that most problems can be solved by asking "why" five times — sometimes even less — and getting to the root issue.

Say you feel guilty because you've not been saying "Hi" to your colleagues in school. You can utilize the technique like this:

Why do I feel guilty?

Because I don't say Hi to them and it seems unfair.

Why haven't I said Hi to them?

Because I don't even know how to approach them or where to start.

Why is that?

Because I find it hard talking to random people.

Why do you find it hard talking to random people?

Because it seems difficult and I have poor social skills.

See what happened? In less than five whys, we figured out why we are having this HUGE issue. With this, we can tackle and solve this issue easily.

3: Write it all down.

Take everything from steps one and two and write it all down — your guilt, each of the whys you asked, and how you can solve everything. This will help you get a clear understanding of how your mind works when it comes to guilt and problem-solving.

It will also give you a good place to go back to when you decide to finally solve the problem — which brings us to....

4: Take action, and take it tomorrow.

That's right. Once you write everything down, I want you to step back and give it some space.

Do you want to know how to stop procrastinating? It's not by trying to do everything at once.

Because we're humans — and as humans, we are naturally cognitive misers and have limited willpower.

Just doing the five whys and investigating your guilt takes

a lot — so just pick it up later when you're fresh and ready to take action. I suggest setting aside some time in a day or two so you don't keep pushing it off.

The next time you find yourself saying something like "I'll get to it later," stop and evaluate why.

Maybe it's not a priority for you right now. Maybe you just don't want to do it. Both of these thoughts are perfectly fine. You'll save everyone a lot of time and effort by recognizing and acting on what's really going on.

Step 3: Change how you describe yourself

It's amazing how often we shoot ourselves in the foot before we can even get started.

This happens when we say things like, "I can't do that because I'm an XYZ-type of person."

Here's a good example: A while back, a friend of mine was

talking to me about a girl in his office, and he told me, "I can't talk to her because I'm just an introvert."

I actually got sharp with him. My friend didn't realize that the way he described himself became a self-fulfilling prophecy.

And I was guilty of it too! Back when I looked like this, I used to tell people, "I can't come to the party because I do not like much crowd."

And guess what? That became my reality for YEARS.

ACTION STEP: Reframe the way you talk about yourself.

Quit hiding behind BS-descriptions of yourself as reasons for why you don't do things.

That includes things like:

"I can't make friends because I'm an introvert."

"I'm always going to be out of shape because I'm lazy."

"I can't go into a relationship because I don't hang out much."

Instead, focus on building systems that can help you accomplish your goals — which brings us to...

Step 4: Build systems to accomplish goals

I always get questions along the lines of "How do I find motivation?"

A few insights from these questions:

Motivation is undependable. Waiting for motivation to fall from the sky so you can accomplish your goals is a good way to never get anything done. Why? Because THAT WON'T HAPPEN. You can't wait for your "muse" or "inspiration" to strike.

You need to build the right systems instead. If you asked either of the above people, "What are your steps to accomplish those goals?" they would have no idea how to answer you. That's because it's hard. It's not as appealing as waiting for motivation to strike. However, it's a better approach.

So instead of waiting to be "motivated," take your goal and ask yourself, "What does it take to accomplish my goal?"

And I'm not talking about high-level things like "determination" or "teamwork" or whatever else you find on motivational posters. I'm talking about concrete steps to get there. That will help you develop a solid system for accomplishing your goals.

ACTION STEP: Break down your goal into smaller steps.

Let's take a look at a bad goal and compare it with a good one.

BAD GOAL: "I want to make more friends."

This goal is TERRIBLE. How many people have told themselves this and gotten nowhere? This is because it's vague. There's no concrete action to it. There's not even a way to know when you've accomplished the goal.

Now let's take a look at a better way to approach it.

GOOD GOAL: "I want to make at least four friends a month and hangout 4-5 times with them in a month."

LOVE IT. Notice how I'm focused on the process first by starting off with how many friends I'd want to make in a month. Also, it's only 4-5 times of hangout. That isn't too much time to spend with people that matter.

Do this with your own goals. Maybe you want to be more sociable in school or at your office? Start by talking to one person. Maybe you want a scholarship for school? Start by simply checking out a scholarship book at a library. These small steps will lead to BIG results.

And when you're making these systems, I suggest putting it all on a Google Calendar.

I do this with ALL of my goals.

This is a random to-do that I would normally put in the back of my head, and it would never get done. Instead, I added it to my calendar so it always gets done.

If it's not on my calendar, IT DOESN'T EXIST.

Step 5: Reward yourself for your work

Did you know that talking to random people can help you improve your social skills?

Seriously, it CAN.

Also, rewarding yourself after a job well done can help create powerful shifts in your mindset.

Something like getting a drink, and a cold bath after hanging out with your colleagues at the end of the day, for example, is a simple way to ignite the reward centers in your brain and cement the good feelings that are required for a habit to take root.

Note: Rewards plays an important role in helping habits stick.

ACTION STEP: Ask yourself, "What habit do I want to start?" and "What will I do to reward myself for taking action?"

Here are a few suggestions to get you started:

Every 25 minutes of deep work you do, give yourself a five-minute break to do whatever you want.

After you hit a savings goal for the month, buy yourself something you want, like a pair of shoes or a video game.

After you hang out with your friends, take in a few episodes of that Netflix show you've been meaning to check out.

The reward can be anything you want — as long as you genuinely enjoy it.

The truth of procrastinating

If you want to truly stop procrastinating, you have to come to terms with two truths of productivity:

Truth no.1: We all have the same amount of time in the day, so STOP BLAMING TIME (or your lack thereof). It doesn't matter if you're Bill Gates, a busy student or a busy parent. You just need to learn how to manage your time better.

Truth no.2: You don't have to be an emotionless robot in order to stop procrastinating. Focus and time management are about mindsets and simple, yet powerful shifts in how you approach your to-dos.

By adopting the right mindsets, you can create habits that stick instead of struggling to get the simplest of things done.

How To Dominate People

To dominate means to be in control or have the power to defeat.

The ability to dominate people around you is extremely useful in many spheres of life. Whether it's trying to get a resistant woman into bed or getting a potential customer to see you as someone who is more sociable, the art of out-braining the other person is something you'll need.

There are several ways to do this, and the more you use, the better chance you'll have. It's a synergistic effect that builds up until eventually the other person realizes you are the dominant one, stops trying to win, and just gives you what you want.

Here are some of the ways to do it:

1. Have More Conversational Options

There is a saying that goes, "whoever is most flexible controls the communication." In layman's terms, flexibility means the range of your response choices. If you can ask a reframing question, deliberately misinterpret what they said, and logically assert that their statement is wrong, you have far more options than a person who can only respond with "I agree" or "I disagree." You have the bigger arsenal, you have more choice of how to respond, and hence, you are the dominant one.

A related idea is to simply know more about whatever you're talking about than the other person. Whoever has more information wins, because he can pick and choose what to share, in what order, and only give out little bits at a time until he finds the other person's barrier...then brings out the big guns and blasts right through it. You could call this experience, or you could call it knowledge.

2. Persistence

Some people would only buy your product or pay for your service if you are sociable. Some people will not buy no matter what you do or say, and nothing will change that. The skill comes into play with people who want to buy but rationalize all kinds of reasons why they cannot do what you want them to do.

At this point, you have two options. You can say "ok" and back down (i.e., proving that you are the submissive one) or you can persist (demonstrating a belief in the value of your product). You persist by refusing to take "no" for an answer, utilizing a barrage of techniques meant to bring the other person to your point of view without being pushy, rather friendly. The more tools you have, the more you can calibrate the other person's needs to figure out which tools are most appropriate for the job, and this is where Point 1 comes into play.

3. Have Something For Everything

When you've been doing something long enough, whether it's pickup or sales or anything which involves persuasion, there will come a point at which you've heard pretty much everything. Not only have you heard it before, but you've also heard it so many times that you automatically know the best response, since you've had the time and opportunity to practice responses for that exact same scenario, over and over again.

You may still be surprised from time to time, but usually, you know exactly what joke to make, exactly what question to ask, or exactly which idea to probe in order to move the conversation in the direction you want. This is a byproduct of experience, so you need to have hundreds or thousands of similar conversations to get to this place. When you get there, you will casually blow past objections and barriers because you've done it a thousand times before.

4. Listen Carefully

When you listen carefully, you realize that a person will tell you pretty much all you need to know about them to persuade them successfully. If you're selling something and the person tells you they wish they could buy it, but they're putting their kids through school; perfect. Now you know what's important to them: their kids. So you alter your conversation to demonstrate how buying your product helps their kids as well.

People will also tell you, through body language and "charged" emotion, which topics to avoid in order to successfully persuade them. If you mention kink to a girl and she mentions that she was beaten as a child, it's probably not a good idea to ask whether she prefers being choked or spanked. Yes, I know there are exceptions when broken women enjoy replaying their childhood drama, but I'm talking about most of the time here.

By listening carefully, you learn which paths to persist down and which to avoid altogether.

5. Pay Attention

Similar to Point 4, but more nonverbal. You can tell by subtle changes in vocal tone and body language whether what you're doing is working or not. Persisting at something that is obviously boring the other person just makes you seem uncalibrated, while if you have the ability to notice a sudden "perk" of interest, you know to begin persisting down that path insist.

Most people have no idea what signals they're giving off or how completely obvious their preferences are to anyone who's made the effort to notice and study human behavior. Do it enough and you will shock yourself with how powerful your auto-pilot can be sometimes. There will be situations when, for example, you sell something to a person at an inflated price in 1/10th the time it usually takes you to sell it at the normal price. Such times are proof of your hard work, social skill, and experience, and you may not even consciously be able to dissect what you did.

You just did it. You were in that wonderful "flow" state.

These are some ideas you can use to learn how to dominate other people in a more sociable manner. It is far safer for everyone than exerting your will physically, which can lead to fights and injuries. Far easier to disarm people verbally and with body language, paying close attention to figure out where their triggers are as a guide to where to go.

As I mentioned earlier, the more of these you utilize, the more dominant you will be, and the more expertly you will perform whenever a challenge arises.

Dominant Personality Don't Always Show Aggression

People with strong personalities learn how to socialize in two different ways. In this section, I will show you how dominant people function in social situations.

For example, in many species of animals, the leader of the pack is typically really good at social learning, but this is completely the opposite of what we tend to believe with people. For instance, dominant birds follow other birds that make smart decisions.

It's not a surprise when someone with a strong personality gets what they want out of a social situation, but they do it very strategically. They approach it in a way an animal naturally would. Socially dominant people will either make allies and try to sway others onto their side with solid arguments, while aggressively dominant people will use a more dictatorial type of strategy. If you don't agree with the aggressive personality type, it's "my way or the highway".

It's easy to forget that humans are animals, which is why it makes sense researchers can find similar social strategies in the animal kingdom. After they surveyed people to find out their preferences regarding how to act during social situations, they realized there was a pattern. Those who scored high on questions like "I generally put people in contact with each other" were seen as socially dominant. While people who scored high on questions such as "I like it when other persons serve me" represented an aggressive dominance in social settings.

Although aggressively dominant individuals prefer to rely

on their personal experience, well-liked socially dominant individuals are biased toward using information that comes from other people. This shows the positive side of social dominance.

Accurately assessing people's personality types in social settings could be as beneficial as knowing what kind of learner they are. Humans can have so many strengths and weaknesses, and by understanding the full package of a person, students can grow into capable adults more efficiently. People with dominant personalities don't have to be stereotypically uncompromising and bossy. They take control of a situation, are very task oriented, and focused on achieving goals. Just as there must be a leader in a pride of lions, there must be a project manager who naturally, constructively dominates their coworkers.

The more subtle perspective you offer could have important implications for decision-making in both the boardroom and the classroom. For example, if you are trying to help a leader to learn something new it may be important to consider whether they are socially or aggressively dominant and whether they will best learn via a social or individual route.

Building Confidence

Confidence is not something that can be learned like a set of rules; confidence is a state of mind. Positive thinking, practice, training, knowledge and talking to other people are all useful ways to help improve or boost your confidence levels.

Confidence comes from feelings of well-being, acceptance of your body and mind, and belief in your own ability, skills, and experience. Confidence is an attribute that most people would like to possess.

What is Self-Confidence?

Although self-confidence can mean different things to different people, in reality it simply means having faith in yourself.

Confidence is, in part, a result of how we have been brought up and how we've been taught. We learn from others how to think about ourselves and how to behave - these lessons affect what we believe about ourselves and other people. Confidence is also a result of our experiences and how we've learned to react to different situations.

Self-confidence is not a static measure. Our confidence to perform roles and tasks and deal with situations can increase and decrease, and some days we may feel more confident than others.

Low-confidence – This can be a result of many factors including fear of the unknown, criticism, being unhappy with personal appearance (self-esteem), feeling unprepared, poor time-management, lack of knowledge and previous failures. Often when we lack confidence in ourselves, it is because of what we believe others will think of us. Perhaps others will laugh at us or complain or make fun if we make mistake. Thinking like this can prevent us from doing things we want or need to do because we believe that the consequences are too painful or embarrassing.

Over-confidence – This can be a problem if it makes you believe that you can do anything, even if you don't have the necessary skills, abilities, and knowledge to do it well. In such situations, over-confidence can lead to failure. Being overly confident also means you are more likely to come across to other people as arrogant or egotistical. People are much more likely to take pleasure in your failure if you are perceived as arrogant.

Confidence and self-esteem are not the same thing, although they are often linked. Confidence is the term we use to describe how we feel about our ability to perform roles, functions, and tasks. Self-esteem is how we feel about ourselves, the way we look, the way we think - whether or not we feel worthy or valued. People with low self-esteem often also suffer from generally low confidence, but people with good self-esteem can also have low confidence. It is also perfectly possible for people with low self-esteem to be very confident in some areas.

Performing a role or completing a task confidently is not about not making mistakes. Mistakes are inevitable, especially when doing something new. Confidence includes knowing what to do when mistakes come to light and therefore is also about problem-solving and decision making.

In this section, I have provided you with practical advice about things that you can do to build your confidence and be more sociable.

Ways to Improve Confidence

There are two sides to improving confidence. Although the ultimate aim is to feel more confident in yourself and your abilities, it is also worth considering how you can appear more confident to other people. The following list has lots of ideas on how to achieve this.

- **Planning and Preparation**

People often feel less confident about new or potentially difficult situations. Perhaps the most important factor in developing confidence is planning and preparing for the unknown.

Here are two examples:

Example I: If you are applying for a new job, it would be a good idea to prepare for the interview. Plan what you would want to say and think about some of the questions that you may be asked. Practice your answers with friends or colleagues and gain their feedback.

Example II: If you are planning to attend a party with your colleagues, and you'd want it to go well, it would be a very nice idea if you prepare for the party. Make plans on what you'd like to say to people at the party, how your movement is going to be at the party. You do not want to go there and start cracking lame jokes and expect people to see you as someone who's sociable.

There are many other examples of planning. Perhaps you should visit the hairdresser before you go. How are you going to drive to the party and how long will it take to get there? What should you wear? Take control of unknown situations the best you can break down tasks into smaller sub-tasks and plan as many as you can.

In some situations, it may be necessary to also have contingency plans - backup plans if your main plan fails. If you had planned to attend the party with your car but in the evening the car wouldn't start, how would you get there? Being able to react calmly to the unexpected is a sign of confidence.

- **Learning, Knowledge, and Training**

Learning and research can help us to feel more confident about our ability to handle situations, roles, and tasks.

Knowing what to expect and how and why things are done will add to your awareness and usually make you feel more prepared and ultimately more confident.

However, learning and gaining knowledge can sometimes

make us feel less confident about our abilities to perform roles and tasks, and when this happens we need to combine our knowledge with experience. By doing something we have learned a lot about, we put the theory to practice which develops confidence and adds to the learning and comprehension.

First-time lovers to-be may well feel nervous and less

than confident about having a relationship. They are likely to buy books or visit websites which can offer advice and dispel some of the mysteries. They are also likely to talk to other people to gain knowledge and understanding.

The same applies to workers. In the workplace, training may be provided for staff to teach them how to manage or work with new systems and procedures. During a period of organizational change, this is particularly important as many people will naturally resist changes. However, if those affected by the changes are given adequate information and training then such resistances can usually be minimized as the staff feel more prepared and therefore more confident with the new system.

- **Positive Thought**

Positive thought can be a very powerful way of improving confidence.

If you believe that you can achieve something then you are likely to work hard to make sure you do it, however, you don't believe that you can accomplish a task then you are more likely to approach it half-heartedly and therefore be more likely to fail. The trick is convincing yourself that you can do something - with the right help, support, preparedness, and knowledge.

The basic rules of positive thinking are to highlight your strengths and successes and learn from your weaknesses and mistakes. This is a lot easier than it sounds, and we often dwell on things that we are not happy with from our past - making them into bigger issues than they need to be. These negative thoughts can be very damaging to confidence and your ability to achieve goals.

- Try to recondition the way you think about your life

Know your strengths and weaknesses. Write a list of things that you are good at and things that you know need improvement. Discuss your list with friends and family as, inevitably, they will be able to add to the list. Celebrate and develop your strengths and find ways to improve or manage your weaknesses.

We all make mistakes. Don't think of your mistakes as negatives but rather as learning opportunities.

Accept compliments and compliment yourself. When you receive a compliment from somebody else, thank them and ask for more details; what exactly did they like? Recognize your own achievements and celebrate them by rewarding yourself and telling friends and family about them.

Use criticism as a learning experience. Everybody sees the world differently, from their own perspective, and what works for one person may not work for another. Criticism is just the opinion of somebody else. Be assertive when receiving criticism, don't reply in a defensive way or let criticism lower your self-esteem. Listen to the criticism and make sure that you understand what is being said, so you can use criticism as a way to learn and improve.

Try to stay generally cheerful and have a positive outlook on life. Only complain or criticize when necessary and, when you do, do so in a constructive way. Offer others compliments and congratulate them on their successes.

- **Talking to Others and Following Their Lead**

Ideally, this will be someone that you see regularly, a work colleague, a family member or a friend - somebody with a lot of self-confidence who you'd like to mirror. Observe them and notice how they behave when they are being confident. How do they move, how do they speak, what do they say and when? How do they behave when faced with a problem or a mistake? How do they interact with other people and how do others react to them?

If possible, talk to them to learn more about how they think and what makes them tick.

Speaking to and being around people who are confident will usually help you to feel more confident. Learn from others who are successful in fulfilling the tasks and goals that you wish to achieve - let their confidence rub off on you.

Also, as you become more confident, remember to offer help and advice, become a role model for somebody less confident.

- **Experience**

As we successfully complete tasks and goals, our confidence that we can complete the same and similar tasks again increase.

A simple example of this is driving a car.

Most people who have been driving for some time do so almost automatically - they don't have to think about which peddle to push or how to handle a junction in the road, they just do it. This contrasts to a learner driver who will probably feel nervous and have to concentrate hard. The learner lacks experience and therefore confidence in their ability to drive.

Gaining experience and taking the first step can, however, be very difficult. Often the thought of starting something new is worse than actually doing it. This is where preparation, learning and thinking positively can help.

Break roles and tasks down into small achievable goals. Make each one of your goals fit SMART criteria. That is to make goals Specific, Measurable, Attainable, Realistic and Timed.

Whatever you do, aim to become as good as you can. The better you are at doing something the more confident you become.

- **Be Assertive**

Being assertive means standing up for what you believe in and sticking to your principles.

Being assertive also means that you can change your mind if you believe it is the right thing to do, not because you are under pressure from somebody else.

Assertiveness, confidence and self-esteem are all very closely linked - usually people become naturally more assertive as they develop their confidence.

- **Keep Calm**

There is usually a correlation between confidence and calmness.

If you feel confident about a task then you will likely feel calm about doing it. When you feel less confident, you are more likely to be stressed or nervous.

Trying to remain calm, even when you're under stress and pressure, will tend to make you feel more confident.

To do this, it is useful to learn how to relax. Learn at least one relaxation technique that works for you and that you can use if you're feeling stressed. This may be as simple as taking some deliberate deep breaths both in and out.

- **Avoid Arrogance**

Arrogance is detrimental to interpersonal relationships.

As your confidence grows and you become successful, avoid feeling or acting superior to others. Remember - nobody is perfect and there is always more that you can learn. Celebrate your strengths and successes, and recognise your weaknesses and failures. Give others credit for their work - use compliments and praise sincerely. Be courteous and polite, show an interest in what others are doing, ask questions and get involved.

Also, admit to your mistakes and be prepared to laugh at yourself.

Practicing Your Confidence Skills

Confidence can diminish over time if you don't practise your skills or if you hit setbacks. As you become more confident, you should continue to practise your skills to maintain and boost your confidence further.

Set yourself confidence targets that require you to step out of your comfort zone and do things that make you feel a degree of nervousness or apprehension.

Potential confidence targets may include:

- Starting a task or project that you've been putting off for a long time. Often we put off starting important tasks because they seem overwhelming, difficult or awkward to complete. Simply making a start on such a task can boost confidence and make you more inclined to complete it.
- Making a complaint in a restaurant if there is a problem with your order. If you would not usually complain about a problem when doing so is a good way to improve your confidence and assertiveness skills.
- Standing up to ask a question at a public meeting or in a group. By doing this, you are making yourself the centre of attention for a few minutes.
- Volunteering to give a presentation or make a speech. For many people speaking to a group of people is a particularly scary prospect. The best way to overcome this fear and gain confidence is with experience.
- Introducing yourself to somebody new. This could be a place where people have something in common - like at a party or a conference, making it potentially easier to have a conversation. Or you could talk to a complete stranger in a lift/elevator.
- Wearing something that will draw attention - such as a garish colour. Personal appearance is an important factor in self-esteem and people with lower self-esteem tend to try not to be noticed. Make a statement and stand out in a crowd!

- Joining a group or class in your community. You will potentially benefit from lots of different ways by meeting new local people and learning new things while improving your confidence.

- Taking an unfamiliar journey on public transport. Travelling to a new place using an unfamiliar route and with random people will make most people feel at least slightly uncomfortable. But it is a great way to improve confidence.

Now ask yourself; how do I feel about each of the ideas on the list above? Perhaps some gave you minor feelings of butterflies whereas others filled you with dread. Although the list uses common examples of potentially confidence-boosting tasks, some may not be right for you. Think of some confidence targets that are right for you - then start with easier ones and build up.

Building Confidence Plays a Big Role In Improving your Social skills

Social skills and confidence in social settings don't come naturally to everyone, and that's completely okay! We can't all be the life of the party. One of the best confidence tips is to put yourself out there to meet new people and have even just a simple conversation with them as this can develop your ability to ask questions and make a connection. This boost your social skills drastically.

The more you get used to talking to new people, the easier it will become and the more self-confidence you build. You might actually find that you start to feel enjoyment rather than fear in larger and more diverse situations.

Take a Risk Today

If you're really committed to improving your confidence and social skills, why not take a risk! This will mean something different to everyone, as everyone is at a different stage in developing their skills.

For someone, a risk might be a small step such as saying good morning to the person they stand next to at the bus stop every morning. For someone else, a risk could mean inviting a few people out for a coffee to work on interacting with more than one person at once and finding the confidence to speak amongst a group.

Take Action Today!

Make Friends without Giving Up Who You Are

Making new friends without giving up who you are is really hard to do when you don't know how. Who wants to do something just to wind up struggling and failing?

Also, trying to make new friends when you don't know the reasons why you've been struggling to do it is a lot harder.

That is why I have put together this list of 11 reasons you've had some trouble in this part of your life and what to do about it. Once you see where you've been stuck within any of these common holding patterns below, you can more easily change your approach so you can start building a fulfilling social life today. And yes, you do not have to change/give up who you really are before you can make friends.

Here are 10 Reasons You Have Trouble Making New Friends (And What to do About It)

1. You think making friends should "just happen."

Once we graduate from school, there's not a lot of structures in place to help us along in making new friends. We have to be grown-ups and make those opportunities and structures for ourselves.

This is what I suggest.

I suggest that you come up with a strategy that works for you on finding and making new friends, including showing up at places where you figure people with your interests are already hanging out (When you hang out with people with your interest, you do not have to give up who you are). When you do that, you're not leaving things up to chance, but taking steps to go after what you want. Aside from making more friends, just the practice of taking strategic action feels good in and of itself.

2. You haven't realized yet that making friends is like dating.

The process of making new friends is a lot like dating – you meet someone you like, and you schedule a time to see them again.

For whatever reason, scheduling new-friend-dates happens more rarely than it could. It's normal to feel a little shy when initiating getting together again, but the important thing to remember is that when you feel a spark and genuinely enjoy each other, make a date!

3. You're afraid that initiating conversations will come across as creepy.

What you do for a living shouldn't stop you from making friends or honouring invitations. The truth is, if there's genuine mutual interest and it's a gentle invite, it's not creepy! In fact, my friend and I were talking about this some time ago in the context of dating, and she said of men who have this fear, "If you think you're creepy, that means you're not! Because the truly creepy ones have no idea they're being creepy."

This is pretty funny, and there's definitely some truth in there. Better than worrying about whether or not you're being creepy, focus on noticing whether there's genuine mutual interest there and whether the other person is enjoying you. If he/she is, then they'd probably like to see you again too, so it's not creepy to help them have more of what they want. This goes for dating and friend contexts.

4. You forget your friends have other friends like them.

If you're at a loss for where to find new friends, start with the people you love and respect the most. Organize a small get-together, or if your friend loves to do that kind of thing, offer to co-host. Then, even if you each just invite a couple more people, you're making a great opportunity for new friendships all around.

Bonus points that you're now a connector in your friend's eyes (and in reality), so you're an even more attractive person to get to know. Everyone loves a connector, and it's really not hard to do. It all starts with a small get-together or two, bringing folks together.

5. You pressure yourself to like everyone.

If you're a nice person, you like everyone, right? Certainly, you don't NOT like people. This is what I believed most of my life, anyway.

When I realized I can respect everyone and show kindness without doing backflips over getting to spend time with them, I became much happier and more relaxed. It's okay not to like everyone. You can't possibly, so don't try to force it. If you find you like someone, capitalize on that by setting up "dates" and getting to know them better. Soon, you'll have a budding friendship.

Meanwhile, don't stress when you're not into someone.

Still, be kind and respectful, but you're under no obligation to spend time and energy getting to know them if you don't want to. It wouldn't be fair to them anyway. After all, do YOU want anyone befriending you just because they think they should? Yuck, didn't think so.

6. You don't want the chaos and messiness that intimacy can bring.

Don't think that just because you make friends with someone that it's going to be dramatic. It's only dramatic if either (or especially both) of the parties involved are dramatic as well. And you don't have to try being dramatic because your potential friend is dramatic. You can make sure your relationships are full of ease and collaborative by first being an awesome person yourself, and secondly, choosing your friends well.

Be the friend who naturally attracts the kind of friend you want. The same goes for dating, by the way. Be the man/woman who naturally attracts the kind of dates or partner you truly want. YOU DON'T HAVE TO GIVE UP WHO YOU REALLY ARE TO MAKE FRIENDS. NO!

7. You feel shameful about your lack of friends.

When we see ourselves as "not social enough" or inherently undesirable, we don't feel (or look) so hot. Just because you don't have as many dear friends as you'd like now, doesn't mean there's anything wrong with you. It simply means you've not identified exactly what you want in a friend and then gone about becoming a natural, intuitive match for that kind of person, and second, not sought out those folks and invited them on friend-dates.

8. You didn't realize that making friends is 95% SKILL and 5% talent.

Does a little talent help? Good looks? Sure. Do you NEED the 5%? No, you don't. Making yourself a more attractive potential friend is a skill. You can make yourself attractive to the kinds of people you're drawn to by taking great care in your presentation, emotional health and happiness, ambition, and everything else.

Skills are learn-able and build-able, and most of life can be dramatically enhanced with skills alone, regardless of any talent that may or may not be there to offer its tiny 5%. We don't often think of talent as so tiny, but it is compared to the monumental force of skill-building. It's just that most of us don't know how to skill-build very well, so we end up noticing and crediting things to talent much more than is warranted.

9. You're a private person and don't want 55 best friends.

Perfect! You don't have to go nuts and spend every waking moment with folks just because you set up one friend-date. Remember that making friends is an inherently gradual process. You decide what kind of social life you want. It's creative process that is completely up to you, and with time and attention, you can make as many or as few friends as you want. It all boils down to what we want.

10. You've forgotten what you have to offer.

I bet you $250 that you're awesome at something.

Maybe it's something purely social like making people laugh. Maybe it's intellectual or something more strategic, like with your career success. Maybe it's a warmth and cosiness, like baking or homemaking skills.

Whatever you're awesome at can be a GREAT quality to bring to the table in a friendship.

Laughter? That one's obvious. You put people in their happy-endorphin-place.

What about intelligence and success? You can provide reason and objectivity to problems your friends are trying to solve.

Warmth and cosiness? When your friends come to your house, they feel happy, loved, and nourished.

Think about the skills and/or natural disposition you have and how you can start sharing it with new friends.

Then, get cracking at skill-building to fill any missing pieces in your friendship-making process and enjoy what happens.

What You Should Know About Friendship

Friendship is more complex as an adult, especially in your 20's and 30's.

This is the time when people start to make major life decisions like getting married, buying a house or moving across the country to pursue their dreams.

It also happens to be the most important decade for professional success. But a demanding job may limit the time for socializing. Frequent get-togethers may become a thing of the past as you focus on climbing the corporate ladder or leave it behind altogether to blaze an entrepreneurial path.

All of these factors make maintaining relationships–particularly friendships–challenging. Not only is it harder to make new friends when you're crazy busy, but differences in priorities and values may also cause to old bonds to fall apart.

Here's one thing you should know – No matter where your career takes you, relationships are essential to your health and happiness. As you chase your career dreams, you'll inevitably grow personally and professionally. Your friendships will transform as a result.

Keep in mind these four truths to nurture positive connections and reach your professional goals in the process.

- **You Get Out What You Put In**

If someone's friendship means a great deal to you, it's up to both of you to invest time and resources into keeping the flame alive. That might mean getting a regular Skype date on the calendar with your college roommate or being the one to follow up (yet again) to an email.

Avoid keeping score, but if you're the only one demonstrating effort or you sense the relationships is turning toxic, you may need to re-evaluate the connection and consider moving on.

- **Work-Life Balance is an Ongoing Process**

While hanging out after school suited friendship-building as a kid, ample free time is in short order as an adult. That means you have to get creative when trying to adapt your social life around your obligations and responsibilities.

Finding the right work-life balance is a challenge every ambitious person faces, but it's entirely possible to make time for friends even with a chaotic schedule. You can actually put your business skills to work outside of the office to negotiate healthy boundaries, communicate your needs and win the support of those closest to you as you tackle big goals.

- **Making Friends as an Adult Takes Time**

Opportunities to meet people are everywhere–from the office to industry events, conferences or happy hours. Although you may be interacting with more people, keep in mind that forming deep connections takes time and requires repeated exposure.

Sure, it can be a lengthier process to get to know new colleagues and build rapport, but be patient. If you enjoy someone's company and sense that they return the sentiment, true friendship will come with time as long as you're intentional about growing it.

- **It's Okay to Let Go**

In today's world, the length of time you've been friends with someone does not correlate with the strength of your friendship with that person. What's important is how the relationship makes you feel right now–not when you were two or twelve years old.

Nevertheless, it can hurt when lifelong friends don't support your career decisions or understand what you do for a living. You may struggle with FOMO (Fear of Missing

Out) or feel like you're falling behind while everyone is off accomplishing great things. Emotions like anger, jealousy and resentment can turn toxic and sap your motivation.

How do you know when you're in this situation?

Here's what I advice; do an emotional gut check next time you're with the friend in question or see an update from them on social media. Are you irritated, frustrated, confused, hurt or distant? These red flags can signal it's a good idea to draw the relationship to a close.

Letting a broken relationship fade away if it's not functional or uplifting anymore is not only okay–it's essential to your long-term health and happiness.

Conclusion

The type of social skills that truly improve your life are those that help you get to know other people on a deeper level and help you build real friendships.

Sometimes it's overwhelming to prepare for the future when you aren't even sure what's around the next bend. But don't stress. You now know the ways to prepare for whatever lies ahead even when you don't know what that might be.

Certain life skills—skills you can develop now—will help in almost any situation. They also tend to improve most areas of your life in sometimes obvious, sometimes subtle ways. Bit by bit, you can become more prepared for whatever life throws at you.

These social skills set we've talked about has little to do with popularity.

These skills play a big role in the school, Business, Church callings, dating, meeting your spouse, career, and pretty much everything else you do in life where you might encounter another living person.

For how to improve your social skills, you first have to make this a goal. You have to set your mind to it. This means that you need to learn how to do it, set aside time to practice your skills and make it a point to follow through.

Reading this book won't do it for you automatically. It only gives you the tools that you need to start improving your social skills. Actually using the tools is up to you.

If you work out, you know that when it comes to lifting, if you're not pushing yourself, you're not making changes in your body. The same is true of social skills. If you're not pushing yourself outside of your comfort zone, you're not acquiring the social skills that you want to, the skills that are going to make you highly effective in just about any situation. Remember that getting rid of some of the discomforts that you might have about socializing is part of what you're trying to do by working on your social skills.

There is a significant correlation between your social skills and your success in any area of life. With good social skills, it's easier to make friends, build strong relationships and get ahead in your career.

As someone who lacks social skills, it's essential to follow the steps I have put down in this book, which are:

- Managing Shyness.
- Improving Your Conversations.
- Making Friends Without Giving Up Who You Are.
- Building Genuine Relationships.
- How to Dominate People.
- Body language.
- Stopping procrastination.

Following some (if not all) of the instructions in this book, you will be able to build and improve your social skills in no-time.

As your social skills improve, you'll find yourself feeling more confident in social settings and connecting easier with others. These skills will open up a wide range of opportunities in your life. All you have to do is take advantage of them. Take Action Today. Goodluck!

STORYTELLING

Manipulation of the Audience - Learn How to Skyrocket Your Personal Brand and Online Business Using the Power of Social Media Marketing, Including Instagram, Facebook and YouTube

Daniel Anderson

INTRODUCTION

Everybody and everything has a story. Some of them we study in schools in history classes, some we read for pleasure in the form of a novel, and most of them nowadays we consume in the form of movies, painting, music, architecture, and others. Today, the power of storytelling enters the businesses and becomes an indispensable skill for success.

Story is a narrative account of an event or a sequence of events. It can be true or fictional. But a good story always has a core element of truth, even if it is fiction. The message the story tells must be true. It must be consistent and authentic. A story adds emotion, characters and sensory details to plain facts. That's why a story grabs us, pulls us along its plot and delivers its key message powerfully.

Storytelling is the art to tell stories to engage an audience. The storyteller conveys a message, information, and knowledge, in an entertaining way. Literary techniques and nonverbal language are his tools.

The storytelling comes to us from ancient times. The spoken storytelling was the only way to share the experience of the communities and to get to know the world around at times before the appearance of media. The power of storytelling has been recognized and used by governments. One of the examples is the power of the church in medieval Europe, where the narration of the Bible held the population in fear and obedience. Moreover, the priests have been well known for their rhetoric skills. Even nowadays, in some countries, the content of history books is changed with the new governments getting to power. But the power of storytelling does not necessarily have to be abused. In most cases, the storytelling is used to promote science, and the method is being utilized by marketing as a new wave of product promotion.

In this book, you are going to see the power of stories and storytelling and also learn how to use in the different circumstances in your life.

HAPPY READING!!

CHAPTER 1: STORYTELLING AND ITS IMPORTANCE

Storytelling - A Time-Honored Tradition

Everyone likes a good story. From the olden days when the elderly would gather children and tell of stories of the past, to the modern groups at libraries where authors of books read their stories, storytelling is a time-honored tradition. What makes storytelling so exciting depends on the storyteller. If the storyteller is exciting and entertaining, then you can enjoy every minute of the story. The interesting part of storytelling is that most of the stories told are based on true events. This not only gives you an interesting story; it helps you learn something.

This honored tradition offers many adventures for all to enjoy. Everyone has a grandfather or grandmother who has told you that story of how they were in World War II or that they were part of the Women's right to vote. These stories not only offer knowledge and learning; they are part of your history. Learning about your ancestors through your immediate family is part of genealogy. Storytelling offers this much and more. Everyone likes to sit around and listen to their relative tell them about these types of stories. It gives them a sense of purpose because more often than not, stories always have a moral to whatever was being told.

Through storytelling there comes a chance of bonding. Bonding with family or friends is an important part of our lives. These are our partners in life, and it is always a good idea to draw knowledge from their experiences. There are times which storytelling is imagined and considered fiction, but because of the storyteller, the story gives entertainment. Having a good storyteller is vital for good storytelling. Many people in today's society forget this time-honored tradition.

Forgetting about storytelling is never a good idea. Without this tradition, there would be more television watching, video game playing, and all together waste of time. It is best to tell as many stories as you can to your children and grandchildren. Remembering this time-honored tradition will improve your attitude to stories.

Stories, Storytelling and the Healing Process

Lewis Carroll, the author of Alice in Wonderland, once called stories "love gifts." The power of stories combined by love provides the foundation for healing on many different levels. There are many in today's societies (worldwide) who have suffered many traumas and therefore need to hear the stories told with loving care. The storyteller, with every telling of healing stories, gives a precious gift. The stories told by the storyteller provide a means fo r people to strengthen themselves and begin to heal.

Sadly, there are many today that would dismiss storytelling as mere entertainment. The argument that the stories cannot possibly be true and that they are a waste of time in today's world of science and technology is commonly cited. Can the stark, clinical environment be a true place of healing? Is there a place in the modern world for fairy tales, legends, and other stories?

Storytelling is almost the oldest art in the world, the first conscious form of literary communication. In many cultures, it still survives, and it is not an uncommon thing to see a crowd held by the simple telling of a story.

There are signs of a growing interest in this ancient art, and we may yet live to see the renaissance of the storyteller and the troubadour. One of the surest signs of a belief in the educational and healing powers of stories and storytelling is its introduction into the therapy methods available to doctors, educators, and clergy. It is just at the time when the imagination is most keen, the mind being unhampered by the collection of facts, that stories appeal most vividly and are retained for all time.

Long before pen was set to paper, fairy tales, legends, and stories existed as a means to transfer knowledge from one generation to another. Spreading knowledge through stories was both entertaining and educational. Religious leaders throughout time have used many metaphors and parables to teach valuable lessons of morals and ethics. Some 20th-century doctors believed that such stories contained symbolic messages which spoke to the unconscious of the listener. Storytelling creates a bridge between teller and listener across which authentic communication can take place. And it is within this intimacy that the 'healing' or 'therapeutic' aspects of a story lie. Since the beginning of time, stories have helped us discover the meaning in our experiences, offered possible explanations for what we struggle to understand. Stories invite our imaginations and hearts to stretch over the void to reach out to one another.

Stories and storytelling are appropriate for use at any stage of the healing process. Certain processes are common throughout all therapies; notably diagnosis, establishing empathic rapport, and carrying out a treatment plan. The use of stories and storytelling appear to be particularly effective because they are non-threatening, engaging to both the conscious and unconscious, foster independence, bypass natural resistance to change, model flexibility, make the presented ideas more memorable, and mobilize the problem-solving and healing resources of the unconscious (Dr. Milton Erickson, 1976). Stories and storytelling speak to the normal and healthy core of the individual and can be an instrument of long-lasting and permanent changes.

Storytelling is a sharing experience. When a storyteller shares a story, they show a willingness to be vulnerable, to share ideas and feelings. That kind of sensitivity invites people to listen with open minds and hearts. Enjoying a story together creates a common experience. Storytelling, properly done creates a relaxed, restful feeling. It establishes an environment for the listener to feel comfortable and begin the healing process.

The most powerful and effective way of presenting stories is to tell from the heart and to engage the listener. In this way, the stories and storytelling become an integral part of the healing process.

Storytelling - Skills of the Ancients for Business Success Today

Storytelling has been ingrained in our society and our humanity since the dawn of time. Parents and grandparents have always told stories that embodied their culture. The wisdom of the ancients is captured and passed on in the story. Most great religious texts contain some form of a story. In business, the value of this powerful communication medium is only now being realized.

- Forward-thinking leaders realize the best way to articulate their vision and values is in stories.

- Clever communicators are aware that embedding a key point in a story is the most likely way it will be heard and retained.

- Smart salespeople know that the best way to deal with a client objection is to tell a story about a similar client.

Not a Fairytale... a Fable

Much of the resistance to storytelling in business came from the perception that it's childish - "Storytelling - that's what do with my kids!" It's because we learned some of our earliest lessons through the story - before we could even read - that the story format is so powerful.

Now in business, we're not telling fairy-tales - fanciful

stories designed to entertain and amuse. What we are telling are mo re like fables - short stories with a message at the end.

The format remains the same. While you might not start with the words, "Once upon a time in a land far far away..." if you start your business story by mentioning the time and place it will have more credibility. You probably won't end with, "... and they all lived happily ever after!" But, if you're telling a story to a client to have them change their mind, then you'll only do this with a happy ending!

The 'Great' Story

History is made by the great stories: brave humans who overcame adversity to inspire the world. The stories of Nelson Mandela, Lim Bo Seng, and Malala Yousafzai should be known by every school child. But, in business, these stories, while inspirational, will often fail to get the changed attitude or behavior that we seek. This is because these individuals are so exceptional that most of us can't relate to them. So, the most effective stories are often not the "inspirational hero" stories, but the everyday stories that they can relate to.

Put them in the Story

The most effective story is where the listener can easily imagine themselves as one of the characters. It is a situation similar to one they have experienced previously. This makes it easy for them to put themselves in the story. They create the scene in their mind faster; they are engaged more because it seems so 'real'; but, most importantly of all, they are more likely to see the message of the story as being relevant to them.

The Business Story - Same but Different

Some people say, "I haven't got time to tell stories. My clients say they are busy and they just want the information. They will get annoyed at me if I start telling them stories." This is understandable. Three points to remember:

1. **Give them what they need to know** - not just what they are asking for. Sometimes there are issues, implications, consequences that they need to understand and the most effective (and efficient) way to do this is through a story.

2. **Be time sensitive.** A business story needs to be shorter. So, you use only the bare minimum in set-up and narrative so they will understand the message. This is why success in business stories can often be dependent on your choice of story. If it takes too long to explain in the set-up, then it won't work because you will have lost them before they see the relevance.

3. **Don't 'signpost' your story.** Whatever you do, don't start with, "Let me tell you a story." They will switch off. Just start the straight in, "I had a client in a similar situation just last month." You'll have them hooked straight away - and they want to find out what happens.

Storytelling is ancient, but that doesn't mean it's out of date. In today's noisy, information-overloaded business world, being heard and remembered is harder than ever. Using the ancient art of storytelling to create cut-through for your message will give your business the edge!

What is Corporate Storytelling?

Corporate storytelling is becoming a new essential leadership skill. It can be used in training and development or succession planning. Through narrative stories, storytelling shares a story about a business challenge, success or experience, while imparting the values and skills of the storyteller.

Storytelling creates an opportunity for active listening, reflection, and dialogue. Stephen Denning, author of The Leader's Guide to Storytelling, states the following seven objectives for storytellers:

1. Communicate a complex idea and spark action.
2. Communicate who you are.
3. Transmit values.
4. Foster collaboration and cross functionality.
5. Tame the grapevine or neutralize negativity.
6. Share knowledge, information, and wisdom.
7. Lead people into the future.

Storytelling is very different from a lecture focused session. Stories should be presented in a plain, simple conversational and direct style. PowerPoint slides or overheads only distract from the story. After finishing a story, the storyteller or facilitator should invite listeners into the discussion to create a learning environment that shares individual insights and reactions. Listeners should be asked what was learned from the story based on its outcome. Was there success or failure in the story? What can be taken away from the story for a better understanding of how to respond to a similar or different situation within the organization at a later time.

Storytelling is the personal delivery of a case study. The context already exists and does not require building scenarios or simulating the work environment - it is the storyteller's experience retold. To create a personal story, first choose your story by asking yourself these questions:

- What story do I want to tell?
- What do I want to convey?
- What organizational outcomes do I hope to create as a result of my story?

Next, develop your story by creating an outline that can answer these questions:

1. What is the theme of my story?
2. What is the sequence of events in my story?
3. What lessons were learned to help improve the organization?

Storytelling can deliver powerful learning. Is your organization ready to try telling some of its stories?

Storytelling - How Important Is It To Your Brand?

In this 21st Century, there are stories everywhere, more so than before. On television. In newspapers and magazines. Online. Offline. Everywhere we look and see; there is a story. Enhanced by various tools of technological; stories, whether true or 'fake' news, now move more rapidly. They are traversing communities and countries within seconds. Within this quickly changing information environment, for businesses, companies or corporations need to find a way which enables them and their products to stand-out amidst the noise. Therefore, having the "right" story to promote their brand, helps. As an ancient art form, storytelling narrates traditional, cultural and social norms providing communities and countries to express through various mediums. Using the vital elements of plot, characterization and narrative point of view storytelling is used in many ways, as demonstrated through various genres: whether written, theatre, film or video, poetry or music, magazine or newspaper. Compelling, emotional, motivational, inspiring, negative or positive, a story can move the reader or watcher from and through various psychological states.

As storytelling is not new and in business more and in today's business environment some organizations are mastering the ability to tell tales on digital platforms, resulting in positive outcomes on their bottom-line. Creating a connection with businesses and customers, regardless of demographics, the love of a story enables people to make a connection with the narrative.

Therefore, with this connection or 'brand storytelling' will help to transform any content marketing strategy, enabling the content's power to easily engage their audience. It is advisable to invest in telling a story and according to Monte Lutz of Edelman Digital, "as companies begin to adjust to the real-time nature of content marketing, it's easy to lose track of your core brand narrative."

Social media has pushed content to be more authentic and transparent and personal, and storytelling is a part of this swing since at a stories core is a great story that engages the business client or customer's emotions recreating an experience for the audience.

There are many corporate storytelling examples which prove how storytelling can be powerful when done good and well. Emotions sell. Oz Content states: Studies show positive emotions toward a brand have a far greater influence on consumer loyalty than trust and other judgments based on attributes. Advertising research reveals emotional responses to an ad have a far greater influence on decisions than the ad's content - by a factor of 3-to-1 for television and 2-to-1 for print ads. According to Oz, there are eleven great and powerful storytelling examples: Weight Watchers, Guinness, Apple, Google, John Deere, Nike, Lego, Airbnb, Harry's, Warby Parker and Dove.

So how does one create the best brand ever?

- Create the right story by ensuring there is value in the 'human element' content.
- Making stories sincere and real.
- The importance of having a Point of View (POV) from the target groups perspective.
- Have an awareness of what connects with potential and present customers.
- Defining and identifying positive protagonists, victors, and heroes within the storytelling.
- Keep the storytelling simple, by being able to tell a story in one line.

Finding the human element in a story helps to connect customers to a brand, company or product, so creating a story around that shows how their lives can be better, connecting them at an emotional level.

In today's world, emotional-connecting storytelling content is king resulting in brand awareness and enabling an enhanced bottom-line.

The Art of Storytelling to Create Powerful Brands

"To connect to people at the deepest level, you need stories."

Rob McKee

Stories are like viruses.

They are ubiquitous - we all 'get' stories, no matter where we're from. They are contagious - tell a story to someone, and if it resonates it'll spread; the most powerful stories demand to be retold, again and again. And they stick - through the re-telling, they embed themselves in our own and our shared memory.

Anthropologists believe that we've been telling stories for as long as we could speak - they're hard-wired into our brains. They bring communities together, and are our primary way to share understanding and transfer knowledge; that's why they work with children - they intuitively seem to realize their importance, which is why children are so transfixed by them.

We are surrounded by stories - in the media, on TV, the books on our shelves, the memories we share. We tell our friends what happened yesterday or last week, or when we were on holiday, and we're telling a story. Anyone who has put a child to bed at night will know how much they beg for a bedtime story, even one they have heard a hundred times; they are drawn to them, mesmerized by them, feeling that there is something intuitively important about them.

There's an obvious link here with branding. Marketing is essentially about telling stories about the products that we make. Consumers have always subconsciously told stories about the brands they interact with - you just have to sit in focus group, and it's all around you: listen to the way they recount what a product does, how they describe when they last used it, what a brand means to them or what it has told them about itself.

It's a buzz word now to talk about 'brand storytelling', but look below the hype, and you'll see that it's often simply lip-service, sprayed on; scratch too hard and it'll come off. Since the invention of the brand positioning model, we have created brands in rational and rigid semantic structures, focusing on adjectives and adverbs, most of which are the product of hours of argument over Roget's Thesaurus. Stories take you on an emotional journey, and if we want a consumer to connect emotionally to a brand, a story will resonate more deeply than a set of out-of-context words.

Let's look more closely at what the experts on stories and storytelling have to say about how you create great stories and see what we can learn about making great brand stories.

Critical element of a story is the 'plot'. Things happen in stories. As you watch, read or listen, the story unfolds through a series of actions and events, which drive the story forward to its conclusion. My old Improve teacher used to make us walk forwards when we were improvising a story for us to physically feel the story progressing. 'Story is a metaphor for life, and life is lived in time,' says Rob McKee. Joseph Campbell studied myths around the world and distilled to their most basic elements. A story consists of Order, Chaos, Resolution: everything is fine in the world of the protagonist; something happens to throw things out of kilter; then, after trials and tribulations, things get (relatively) back to normal again.

Story's sense of progression can be seen implicitly in brands - they help us attain something better than we had before. The message or promise at the heart of the brand needs to echo this. Johnnie Walker is a classic example of this: personal progress, drive & ambition are key to this brand; the striding man symbolizes this. Compare Johnnie Walker, about progress, to Chivas, which reflects the status that you have already attained: static. Imagine a film or a novel, where the hero has already achieved what he needed to do - where can the story go from there? He has nothing to do, to show, to experience. So, all brands need to have a sense of progression innate to them - they have to help move us from one state to another, but they also have to evolve in themselves.

The plot captures the activity within the story in a succession of actions and reactions. There have been several books and articles published that explore 'plot,' the premise of many of them being that there are only a limited number of plot types. The most recent has been by Christopher Booker, who believes that every story that has ever been told falls into one of 7 buckets: overcoming the monster; rags to riches; the quest; voyage and return;

comedy; tragedy; rebirth. If stories are there to teach you, then each plot represents a different human value and analogously teaches us the consequences of different choices and decisions.

If there are only seven different storylines and every story we've ever told is but a version of one of them, then it would follow that there are only really seven brand story types (which surely would seem to make differentiation difficult, but look at the plethora of Hollywood films that adopt each plot type but dress it up in a different, and sometimes unique, way...) In the same way that Booker professes that storytellers can make their stories stronger by embracing their 'type' (and in some way conforming to the structure and process that it sets out), a brand owner can make their brand story stronger by closely mirroring the construct of their story structure.

Here are a couple of examples of brands that have great stories behind them and which embrace their plot type.

Nike has a strong story of challenging yourself, of striving for your best performance and being committed to the passion for that achievement. For Nike, the only thing to get in your way of achieving this is yourself - the limits of your condition, of your stamina and ultimately of your confidence in yourself. What Nike tries to teach us is that there will be times when it will be difficult, it will hurt, you'll want to give up, but you have to fight through it to win the ultimate battle. Nike's story is of 'overcoming the monster' (just like Jaws, like most Bond films, like Michael Clayton, who overcomes the corporate system...). The monster to overcome is the monster inside you.

The Voyage and Return story teaches us that sometimes life takes us to places that might seem amazing and perfect, but ultimately are ruled by false Gods. Dorothy in the Wizard of Oz is mesmerized by the colorful yellow brick road, but realizes that her life is really at home; Andy, the naïve girl in The Devil Wears Prada, ends up rejecting the false world of fashion that had so completely lured her and taken over how she saw the world. This is Dove's brand story. From its Real Beauty platform, Dove tells us to be wary and distrustful of the beauty industry, and that true beauty is owned and defined by you-you don't have to pretend to be someone you're not. The same way that Andy had to look inside herself and judge whether she was true to herself, so Dove persuades its consumers to be true to themselves.

Other examples: Rags to Riches can be seen in Beetle, Quest in J ohnnie Walker, Comedy in WKD or Budweiser, Rebirth in Smirnoff.

To find your brand story, look back at the history of your brand and find the values that are at its core. Look at how and what your brand communicates now. What is the lesson that it is trying to teach its consumers? What is the meaning that lies deep within? Identify which plot type it falls within to make it stronger.

Looking at the 'plot' of your brand can also help to define where your brand is ultimately going, and what obstacles and challenges it might need to overcome.

There is another element that is critical to making good stories: Emotion. "A good story taps into the intellect and emotions of the audience; it leaves listeners enriched in their learning and feelings" (Kaye & Jacobson, 1999). This is what is at the heart of a story - it takes its viewers or readers on a journey, playing with our emotions as we follow the protagonist through his journey. We feel happy when he feels happy; our emotions are plunged when he thinks he's failed; we feel the fear he feels. And a story has to end on an emotional high, something to pay us back for the time that we have invested in it. Likewise, brand stories need to be emotional to connect with your consumers on a deeper, more visceral level. Powerful brands are founded on clear and emotive ideas, and find the emotions behind the brand story, evoking them through all their communications. Think how Cadbury, instead of talking about the joy and pleasure of the product, enacts and shows us joy with the gorilla playing Phil Collins. Think about how O2 is communicating emotionally through its 'We're better connected' platform. ING is moving from telling you about interest rates to showing how fun and playful saving is. Not all emotions are positive... Of the six 'primary emotions' (the ones that anthropologists believe are innate to humans rather than culturally defined) most are negative (sadness, fear, disgust, anger, surprise - positive ones are Joy and Surprise, though this can cross either side). Adverts tend only to show happy people, so what happens when brands center on the other emotions... Marmite showing disgust is probably the best example.

How a brand can succeed and gain a competitive advantage is by telling, and embodying, powerful stories that connect emotionally. If you cannot tell a compelling story about how a product you are designing will be used and the value it will bring to the people who use is, you should question why it is being built in the first place. But, your brand story is not just an anecdote - a few statements and a witty sign-off at the end; stories are metaphors for meaning - they have a 'point' to make. So, your brand story is the sum of all the meaning, character and emotion of your brand.

If you can write a compelling brand story, if you can describe where your brand is going, what it stands for and why it will be what it will be you will build a brand people will connect with, remember & share.

DANIEL ANDERSON

The Importance of Storytelling in Content Marketing

Despite all the distractions of modern life there's nothing we enjoy better than a good story, a skill practically all of us learn at a young age, whether from our parents, grandparents, teachers, and peers, delivered to us sat around a camp-fire, in a lecture hall, over a pint of the good stuff with friends or by way of an immersive IMAX 3D experience, good stories always stick.

With the rise and rise of social media interaction corporations are increasingly required to create compelling 'shareable' content to feed the demand from an increasing number of channels that consumers are using to find and interact with the labels, products, and services they demand. To this end, the art of storytelling is fast becoming a fundamental part of how you can successfully engage with your customers and cultivate your following.

In the pursuit of the perfect narrative, scientific research is delving into the history and the finer details of how good stories can and do change our attitudes, beliefs, and behaviors, and why our brain loves a good yarn.

The importance of storytelling lies in its power to explain, and our brains have long been wired to look for the story when making sense of the world around us. In ancient civilizations those that could explain and most notably embellish the actions of the Gods in times of flood, famine, and war would draw the largest and most attentive audiences, helping to elevate their positions in society and assume positions of authority, thus the rise of priests, judges, rulers and ultimately Alan Sugar, sorry business leaders.

For those in business, today stories can be told using video, arguably the single most engaging format for audiences and one that's fast becoming the preferred way to absorb information. But there's more to just telling a good story than high definition video - if you want a narrative that'll elevate your brand, motivate, inspire and help spread your message the key is in our biology, in particular, the hormone oxytocin.

Oxytocin is a powerful neurotransmitter most commonly associated with relationship building and parent-child bonding. It is produced when we are trusted and shown kindness from others; it helps to motivate us to cooperate with others by enhancing a sense of empathy. Research carried out in the U.S. that involved accurately measuring oxytocin release aimed to understand more about the neurobiology of storytelling and why stories can motivate voluntary cooperation.

Results showed that for stories to motivate people to cooperate in helping others they must maintain attention by building tension during the narrative; if they are successful in doing this they'll not only be more likely to stimulate empathy with the characters but for their audience to mimic the feelings and behaviors of those characters when the story ends. This explains why people are more willing to donate money having watched a charity video.

With an increasing number of businesses making use of video, the neurobiology of storytelling is particularly relevant when understanding what will successfully drive and engage your audience. Wrapping your companies USP's in character driven narrative that can display how you can, or have improved the lives of the characters will help to stimulate empathy from your viewers resulting in a much better understanding of those key messages. Furthermore, they will remember them for longer.

Many brands and organizations have already seen the benefits of how compelling a well-constructed narrative can be upon a target audience, from encouraging people to give generously on Red Nose Day to tell the tale of a startup business. If you want to motivate, persuade and be remembered start with a story of human struggle and eventual triumph. This is what will capture people's hearts - by first attracting their brains.

Despite the many distractions that vie for our attention there's nothing we enjoy better than a good story. Here we look at the hold that stories have over our brains and why marketers are increasingly using the power of storytelling to engage us.

Why is Storytelling Important in Marketing?

Marketing is more than communicating brand messages to audiences, It is a way of engaging with audiences in a way that best appeals to them and allows them to get involved in your brand's journey.

The concept of a brand personality isn't new. Every good brand DNA includes a sense of personality the brand would have if it were a person and if a brand has human-like characteristics, chances are that person has a story to tell. The trick is to find a way to be able to tell that story instead of merely communicating a promotion or sale when you have one.

Brand's marketing or communications team needs to comprise of good storytellers that know how to create greater consumer involvement through emotional engagement. Communicating a sale is ashort-term tactic, while powerful storytelling is the way to create a long-term relationship between the brand and consumer. Humans are connected to each other by their storylines and the point is to find a way for your brand story, and the consumer's one, to meet and move forward together. We are drawn far more to the emotional than the pragmatic, irrespective of what we'd like others to think. Understanding this key human insight will help you build more powerful narratives that connect with audiences more effectively.

Here are few storytelling tips to get you started on your adventure:

1. Be Honest

While it is essential to be able to craft and tell a story right, you need to be telling an honest one. Be consistent and persistent in that truth and build narratives that stay close to your brand promise and DNA - you don't want to confuse your customers by telling a different story each time you communicate with them. Instead, make it as true as you possibly can to a continuing adventure.

2. Be Personal

Storytelling in marketing is very different to conventional advertising. It isn't a sales pitch. You need to first identify and create the persona your brand stands for and put him or her in the centre of the action or plot. You can't tell a boring story, you need to take your consumers on a journey with you and they can only do that if they know who they are following.

3. Be Likeable

If you know your audience, then you ought to know the kind of people they like, and ideally your brand personality needs to incorporate these characteristics. If you want them to root for you, you have to make them like you. Maybe even build in your consumer's personal struggles into the narrative so they can relate to your personality's journey and want to know the rest of the story.

4. Be Linear

If you are telling a story then it ideally needs to have a

beginning, a center point and an end as with all good narratives. Open strong to establish your storyline, set up your character's problem in the middle, and ensure that you come to a solution at the end.

The Power of Storytelling

Every day as we are building our businesses, we all know the key to a successful presentation is a product being sold to the end-line consumer and sponsoring a new person. In an upcoming issue, I am going to write about the difference between making a sale and having customer loyalty in the sales process. In the sales process, you are fighting many different types of animals. For most of those who are in direct sales, you have 45 minutes to present a product/business concept and make a person believe in you, your product, and more importantly have them make a decision that they want what you are offering.

When you are presenting the business, it is very easy for you to get very factual and completely lose the interest of your prospect. When you tell a story about the success of someone who is using the product or have a person give a live testimonial about how much they love being a distributor, you will keep the interest of new people who are listening for the first time. For most of us, the first time in our lives that we were ever presented with the concept of a live audience was back in kindergarten when we played "show and tell." Everyone was always interested in what you were saying because you were simply telling a story. We have all heard of the famous K.I.S.S. rule: Keep It Simple Stupid. When presenting your business or product, the key play is to tell a story and keep it simple. Everyone can relate to the grandmother, who can talk about their grandchild as the most beautiful, precious child in the world. She will make you feel as if her grandchild would be such a gift to own as your own. You need to take that same simplicity and utilize it during your presentation and create the same result - ownership of your product. As you tell stories, people will remember those stories versus all the facts in the world.

"FACTS TELL, BUT STORIES SELL." They should want to get involved in your business or purchase your product because of all of the success stories that you told. People love to be part of a winning team. Storytelling keeps people tied into you and your presentation. I always say when in doubt during a presentation, tell a story to bring people's attention back to you. When I present, I ALWAYS tell many stories because when I was first introduced to direct sales, what perked my ears was a story of a young lady who had a lifestyle I wanted. The personal story of her lifestyle is what made me decide to get involved in the business. In that business, I went on to build an enormous organization, and all I did was tell my story and tell the company's story over and over! storytelling can achieve.

Combining the key strategy of along with the correct mindset, you your wildest dreams!

CHAPTER 2: USING STORY TELLING FOR EFFECTIVE PRESENTATION

The Art of a Presentation

Presentation is a generic term that includes every time someone tells something. It could be a formal presentation to boss and colleagues with the support of technology or can be a story told to friends in a pub. Considering the actual crisis, it could also be a presentation of a job seeker to the Human Resources department of the ideal company. Or a salesperson who has to convince a customer that is the product is the best in the world; even it is not true!

In every situation, the following elements should be mixed and used in different proportions, but every time it is important to use them. One of the best public speakers is Steve Jobs who can use some features to create an effective presentation. In this part of the book, there are highlighted the most popular secrets (most popular and secrets?!?) that are used to present our story, whatever it is.

First of all, it is normal to see persons who are great to tell stories, and then they are not able to say a single word when the boss comes. Or people who could sell a refrigerator in the North Pole, but they are not able to talk to a girl. The good news is that everybody can learn how to do a convincing presentation. To have a prove of that, just check Steve Jobs in his presentation at the university talking about his life and health diseases, where everyone was crying full of emotions and his first presentations decades ago, where everyone was crying but for the horror! After that, everyone can feel better.

Generally, a couple of messages should pass in a presentation: to inform and to entertain. So, it is important to consider what it is said as well as how it is said.

Plan the story

The first step is to be prepared. Planning the plot of the story with analogical support gives the possibility to check the single parts of the story. To do that, software supports are useful, but paper and pens, pencils with different colors and mind maps are much better. The explanation goes more in the mind that is more stimulated the emotional part. Planning a presentation also gives the possibility to insert into it all the possible elements to get the audience attention active. This is the time when it is possible to consider the use of demonstrations, video clips, slides, and every other external element.

The main message

Presentations are used to be remembered by others. Therefore the main message should be clear and easy to remember. To do that a short message is more influenced. TV spots usually use this approach, and some short sentences from the advertisements are commonly used in normal life. Just think a few minutes, and you will be able to think a lot of them. The characteristic they have in common is they are short. We can compare the length as sms or a Twitter message. Even if your message is not told by thousands of people, it must be associated with what you want to say. "The world's thinnest notebook" fits perfectly to MacBook Air.

The story

Like comedians or writers, a presentation is about a story that needs a hero and an antagonist. In this way, the listener can identify himself/herself with the hero and can fell the possibility to fight against the evil. Again, just think to some movies to have a clear example of that. Steve Jobs used IBM as the antagonist in one of his presentation, and Apple was a new force that could save the world.

Audience benefits

The message must have a benefit for who is listening. It could be the best presentation, but if the public is not interested in it, no one will listen. Therefore, the message should be tailored around the audience, and in particular, around the benefit, they can get out of that. It is not interesting for customers that the iPhone can make Apple incredibly reach, popular with a huge market share (that's more important for Apple management). Customers can be attracted by the benefit for them that the iPhone is twice as fast at half of the price.

Rule of the three

Once again, writers use to divide their stories into three parts. It helps to keep the attention high, and it is a good number to remember. Steve Jobs used this rule in his presentation about his life, and everybody can remember those three stories.

Logical plus emotional

It depends on the audience, of course. In any case, a good mix of both should be used. Everybody is impressed by numbers and rational facts, and the emotional factor is usually the winning one. The presentation should convince others with facts: for example, our product is the fastest. And customers must have a good feeling about that, or us. Sometimes a pair of jeans is nice, but we don't buy it because the clerk is not polite. Even more, Steve Jobs likes to sell dreams, not products. It could be like Martin Luther King. In any case, it works, and it is easier to remember. An example could be: "in our small way, we are going to make the world a better place."

Visual impact

Words are important, and images can communicate lots of them in one moment. Even more, a picture can evoke different feelings in the audience. Is the Apple MacBook Air incredible thin? A picture with the Macbook fitting into an envelope is much more powerful. And easier to remember: it has more impact.

Numbers for the audience

Numbers are important because they access to the logical part of the mind. In any case, they must be adapted to the audience. Two hundred twenty million iPods is a meaningful number for sales, not for the customers. 73% of the market share for iPods gives the customers the feeling they are buying the most used product in the market. No number is right or wrong in absolute: it simply depends on the audience.

The emotionally charged event

In every presentation there should be the most important moment, the one everybody will remember. It must be introduced with a sense of suspense, and then the main message should be launched. Prepare your audience to listen to it, or to see that.

Practice makes it perfect

Training is the secret of everything. The first time could be fine; the next will be better. Steve Jobs is an example of that.

Every time there is the possibility to show a presentation. It could be a story or us or our product, whatever. We should be ready at that moment and keep the attention high. Some rules are useful to frame our presentation in a way that will be better remembered by the audience. That's a challenge, but everyone can improve himself/herself getting great results.

The Ws of Effective Presentation

Making a presentation or speaking in public can be a daunting task if not impossible. Even professional public speakers talk about incertitude, nervousness and anxiety every time they have to address an audience. If people who have adopted presentations as their main occupation feel nervous before every presentation, then for the first timer getting the creeps should not be surprising. Most of the uncertainty emanates from what the reaction of the audience will be.

Find below my 5 Ws for making an effective presentation. Indeed there are different ways for calming oneself down before a presentation. This write up, however, is not meant to teach you about handling your nerves before a presentation; this is meant to help prepare adequately for the presentation. The objective is to help boost your confidence and indirectly calm you down for a killer presentation.

The Why:

The first question to ask every time you are asked to make a presentation is to ask why. Why am I making this presentation? You should take time to explore and to understand why you have been asked to speak. There are different reasons for making a presentation. So stop and ask yourself, why you? It may be because it forms part of your work- Job description or that you are an expert in a subject area and so you need to impart knowledge. Answering the why question provides you with a context to which you tailor your presentation. Do you need to inform? Do you need to persuade? Do you need to sell? Maybe you need to teach! Do you need to entertain? Etc. This question must be very clear in your mind. Once you tackle this question, you should be able to structure your presentation to suit the request. This way you are very clear about the agenda, and then you can adequately research to reflect the expectations in the request.

The Who:

To most people, 'the who' part is the most important W among the lot, and it is the one that bothers them. Indeed, 'the who' determines to a large extent how successful or otherwise a presentation is. One important question to ask when asked to make a presentation is to ask who your audience will be. Who am I speaking to? One can have the right words, the right atmosphere, even the right presentation equipment but the effectiveness of the presentation would only be measured by the reaction of the audience. Your presentation must be pitched at the right level for the right audience. The language must be well structured to the understanding of your audience.

Typical example is where a University professor presents two different papers on the same subject to two different audiences. A presentation to his peers on the same subject will differ significantly from a presentation to his students. The question also determines the approach and the tools used in the presentation. The underlying principle is that a presentation is a two-way affair, from the presenter to the audience and from the audience to the presenter. A well-designed presentation, delivered with expertise and skill, crystal clear style, with wit and humor, with the most comprehensive visual aid delivered in the most serene atmosphere will be as dull as dishwater if presented to the wrong audience. Therefore to adequately prepare for a presentation you have to consider the recipient of the message. Ask yourself; who am I speaking to? Who will be in the audience? What do they know about the subject? How many are they? Then tailor your presentation to suit your audience. Research into their background and as much as possible speak to their understanding, not above their heads, neither should you talk down at them.

The What:

The what question addresses your objective. What do you want to achieve with the presentation? It allows you to customize your presentation to address your objectives and the results. To give a good presentation, you need to define what you want to achieve. You can only measure the success of your presentation when you have an objective to which you aim your presentation. It means, giving yourself a goal to measure yourself by. Your objective should be your central message to which other points go to buttress. Defining your objectives also guides the details of your presentation, and you can personalize it to draw out the results. Your objective in a presentation may be to provoke an emotion, to a sales team that has not met its sales target- you inspire, to appeal to your audience for them to release funds, to promote a discussion, etc. Set out your objectives within the four pillars of communication; to inform, to request for an action, to persuade and to build a relationship. The what part provides the framework within which you set out your presentation, and it gives you a yardstick for measuring its effectiveness.

What do you want your audience to do when you finish your presentation. That is your results. Your results must be specific; it must be clear in your mind and must be set out right at the beginning when you prepare for the presentation.

The Where:

The where part of the preparation is pretty self-explanatory. It has to do with location; the arrangement and structure of the venue. You should have a clear picture of what the venue and the arrangement will be. Will you be expected to address the audience in a classroom format, is it arranged to encourage teamwork among the audience, is it arranged to encourage question and answer sections, etc. You also have to research to be sure about the equipment at the venue. Would you have access to a public address system or not? What about a projector, a flip chart, etc.? The nature of the venue also affects your presentation style. You should, therefore, have prior knowledge of the arrangement before the actual date of the presentation. Make a checklist of your needs and make sure that the location can cater to those needs. Where they can't, strategize effectively to address your needs. Surprises right before the presentation can unnerve you and make you disoriented.

The Words:

The words part has two options. Firstly it has to do with

the content of your presentation. You must make a conscious effort to structure your words effectively to reflect your research and to fit the requirements of the presentation. You have to research and come up with the best. Arrange your presentation in a structure that you can easily remember. Use words that are easy to understand and you can easily remember. Make sure that you are comfortable with your presentation and as much as possible limit yourself to what you know and can explain better.

The second part is more of advice. That words are not enough. Make use of visual aids. This also means that your speech must blend with whatever visual aids you have to provide a clearer understanding. Pictures they say paint a thousand words and using visual aids reduces the monotony of your voice. You can lecture but make room for visuals and take time to explain. You can also use sound or even video to add some variety or better still, to engage your audience.

What Nobody Ever Tells You about Presenting

Most likely, you've heard this advice: people buy from people they trust. The interesting thing is: what do they buy?

The decision to purchase works for tangible and intangible items--across the board. It's not just for products and services. People buy other things based on trust. Specifically, they buy into advice, ideas, recommendations, and suggestions from those who they know and believe.

What makes you believable to people who don't know you already? A well-structured story.

Your story is the backbone of your presentation. But here's the part most experts won't reveal how to build a story that is real, solid, and true how to structure your story to engage any audience-even if you're short on time and only have minutes to share your ideas.

The 'how' of storytelling is crucial in business presenting. If you tell a story that is authentic, you are very believable. People in your audience pay attention, get curious and want to hear more. Even if you're just meeting for the first time, people feel that you are trustworthy...and they are interested in doing business with you.

If you tell a story that doesn't make sense, doesn't feel authentic, people will have the opposite response. They might not know exactly why. But something just doesn't fit.

This leads people to feel things like:

"Something is off."

"What he said just didn't ring true."

"I felt like there was a piece missing."

What's the result of this? People feel skeptical. They get picky about little things. They may be consciously or unconsciously suspicious. They question everything. Not only your story... but also your words, your background, your expertise, and your recommendations.

In other words, things take a long time and may not move forward. This is not what you want to achieve in interviewing for a job, initiating a consulting job, or sealing a sale.

Strong story is like the spine of any presentation. You may be presenting your bio, your background or your consulting project.

Perhaps you're presenting the story of your company, research or training program.

Many executive coaching clients have asked me, "what are the key building blocks for a great story?"

Here's the short answer. Whatever the topic, organize so your story makes sense for your audience. Appeal to their sensibilities with these eight building blocks.

- Grabs Attention from start to finish. An instant connection is a secret to outrageous success.

- Builds Credibility with tangible evidence. From news coverage to press releases to testimonials, share what other people have said about your business.

- Deepens Interest by providing clear benefits for the audience.

- Demonstrates Creativity for solving troubling problems and achieving compelling goals.

- Ignites Desire with a magnetic pull of emotions. Reach deep to find core emotional connection with your audience because people want to do business with people who truly understand them.

- Confirms Authentic sense that you, your company and your solutions are 'the real deal.' People want to get involved with people who are committed and genuine.

- Shows Care for your audience. This is vitally important. People want to feel, hear and see that you care deeply about what matters most to them.

- Inspires Action and decisions. Whether your purpose is to educate, inform, present or sell-action is the outcome.

Structure your business materials and presentations around these eight elements, and your story will have power. Plus, there's an added personal benefit. You'll feel confident, at ease and ready for last-minute presentations.

Imagine the power. A well-built story will boost your business...and your bottom line.

With a logical and creative structure to your story, every presentation is much more powerful. This adds a rush of fresh energy for interactive presentations. The best part? You and your team will feel a boost in confidence...and see a boost in your bottom line results.

A Presentation Tip - Tell a Story

Want to take your presentation skills to the next level? Are you tired of just flipping through PowerPoint slides and boring your audience with data? Start thinking like Aesop and start telling stories.

Presentations based on PowerPoint slides can be deadly, but presentations based on examples, real-life situations and stories can be inspiring and memorable. Most of us can remember dozens of stories from our childhood. A story like, The Tortoise and the Hare from Aesop is a great example. You can never underestimate the power of a good story. Storytellers captivate, motivate and inspire an audience. And great salespeople the world over know and use this power to engage with customers.

The Basic Story Formula

So how do you plan a presentation based on the story and what are the elements of a great business story? It boils down to a simple formula: someone doing something against odds.

Someone can be a person, a company or even a product. The something is an action. And the odds, well, that could be a villain or obstacle or challenge. These are the basic elements of all good stories. Now, how do you put those elements to work?

A Story Needs a Hero or Heroine

Story needs a character we can relate to. Start with describing the main character or actor. This could be someone like Erik Weihenmayer an adventurer who climbed Mount Everest. The character could be a small company struggling to gain market share against a Fortune 500 giant, or a salesperson with a disability like Bill Porter who would not take no for an answer.

Describe a Challenge

One you have introduced your character; explain how this character struggled to achieve something or conquered obstacles against all odds. For mountain climber Erik Weihenmeyer, his challenge is that he is blind! He not only climbs mountains but scuba dives and parachutes out of planes! For Bill Porter, cerebral palsy left him with impaired speech and a pain-wracked body. But that never stopped him for selling in a grueling door-to-door market. The movie of his life, Door to Door, shows how he overcame insurmountable odds to be one of the top salesmen in America.

The best characters and challenges are inspirational, and like Aesop, the audience can see a lesson in the characters as they struggle to succeed. You need to draw that conclusion for your audience: do not assume they will connect the dots on their own.

Relate to Your Audience

The most important part of your story is to make the challenges of the character relevant to your audience. Does your team face obstacles? What could they learn from the determination and resolve of your character? Is the economy a villain working against a small company? What strategy did that company put in place to overcome the economic downturn and succeed? Show your audience HOW they could do the same. Even better, what is your personal story of rising above the odds...your obstacles...your solution? Audiences love a personal story of triumph.

Practice Makes Perfect

Mastering the art of the story can propel your speaking to new heights, but you need to practice. After all, it IS art. Try storytelling regularly in small meetings or staff events to gain feedback on your skills. Get comments on what works and does not. Listen to good storytellers and take mental notes. Keep a journal and fill it with all the great examples of stories that you hear every day.

Present Your Point More Compellingly - Tell a Story

Far from the bedtime stories of childhood or the pop culture of films, novels, and television shows, business presentation may not seem like the appropriate place for a story. After all, business presentations are where we talk about hard facts. Business presentations are where we let the data influence logical decision-making. Business presentations are no place for a story. Or are they?

Why Stories?

People love stories. They can't help themselves. From the days of our ancestors sitting around the campfire to the modern day storytellers on screen, when we listen to a story, we want to know about the people in the story. We want to know what happens next. Think about it. We've all sat through an awful because we had to know how the story ended. Stories draw an audience into your presentation. Being drawn in helps the audience connect better with you and with your message.

Stories help make the abstract more concrete. In business, we often have to deal with concepts that are hard to visualize if we haven't experienced with them ourselves. A story can help create that picture of what the idea looks like in real life. The more concrete we can make an idea and tie it to something our audience already knows, the m ore likely our audience is to understand and to remember our message.

3 Tips for Storytelling in Presentations
Make the stories personal.

When telling stories, talk abo ut thing s you've expe rienced or observed. That's one way to make sure your audience hasn't just read the story on the internet, in a book, etc. Plus because you're the speaker, the audience wants to hear your insights. Telling personal stories gives the audience a glimpse into who you a re and how you think. Stories help them to learn about and like you.

Have a point. When telling a story, be sure to have a point. The story doesn't have to direc tly relate to the subject you're speaking on, but it should have what presentation skills expert Max Dixon ca lls a transfera ble metaphor -- the story needs to have a lesson that illustrates the bigger message you're trying to deliver. The value of the story will be lost if you can't tie the lesson of the story back to the information you provide. So tell the story and make your point.

Include emotions.

When telling the story, including an emotional element tha t will connect with yo ur audience. Business or not, we're all human beings, and emo tions touch us as individuals. While logic may see m the dominate business theme, emotions tie into business decisions too. Adding an emotional element to your story will help strengthen the connection of your audience to your message. The emotion can range from humor to empathy depending on the subject and the point you're trying to make. Regardless of the emotion, sto ries that touch your audience, whether with laughter or tears, will help make your message easier to understand and more memorable.

Business presentation will always contain the fact and figures that help decision makers make the right call. But using stories can cement the business presentation and make it personal. Use the value of stories to help you connect, communicate and contribute to your next business audience.

Presentation Using "Signature Stories"

It is hard to believe that there are still presenters who will start their presentation with, "Thank you. I am so pleased to be here," or they tell a joke that bears no relationship to their topic. Much stronger is the presenter who has developed strong and effective "Signature Stories."

What Is a "Signature Story?"

"Signature Story" belongs to you. It can be a personal story about your own experience or experiences. It can be a story about someone else's experience. It can be an original story that embraces the topic and points of your presentation. Or, it can also be a traditional story or fairy/folk tale that has been updated to fit your presentation. I have used all, and with proper preparation, they have all worked to my benefit.

Why Use "Signature Stories?"

Remembering that our "Signature Stories" need to be riveting and topnotch, we will find that as long as we make them unique and "our own," our listeners will react to us and our stories. Good stories are easily internalized, so we as listeners will be able to think back and remember the points made in the presentation. I also enjoy hearing a good story again and again. I remember and love re-hearing Zig Ziglar's cafeteria story, Jim Rohn's Girl Scout cookie story, and Stephen Covey's use of the traditional "Golden Goose" story.

Developing the Personal "Signature Story"

The advantage of developing and using your own story is that it happened to you. That doesn't mean that it doesn't seem plausible and even bring to mind similar stories that your listeners have experienced -- this is even better because they will relate more to you and your topic. It is OK to embellish a bit, but my warning here is to share your struggles rather than your triumphs. People like to hear about times when you are the "bug" rather than the "windshield."

Don't be afraid to expose some of your weaknesses or fears. I have a story that everyone loves called "Bat in the Bathroom." It gets lots of laughs, and many of my listeners rush up after my presentation to share similar challenges with nature's creatures.

One other caveat about personal "Signature Stories" is that you are not using them for your therapy. I have heard speakers who think they are touching the hearts of their audience when they are making them uncomfortable. I tell a positive story about my son's bout with cancer, but it took me several years before I could tell it without crying. Once I had control and started to tell it -- it is called, "I Believe in Miracles" -- I have had many relatives of cancer patients thank me for sharing it.

So, get busy and develop your "Signature Story." You will be amazed by the presentation power of using it.

Storytelling: The secret to effective presentation skills

Good presentation is one that inspires your audience keeping them engaged from beginning to end; this, however, is easier said than done. It's natural for our minds to wander; in fact, our minds are wandering more than you might even believe – did you know that on average we have around two thousand daydreams every day? One Harvard study has found that we spend half our waking hours with our heads in the clouds and with each of our little fantasies lasting about 14 seconds, our minds are drifting here, there and everywhere! So, the question is – how can you deliver a presentation that stops minds from wandering? The secret to effective presentation skills lies within storytelling. Storytelling techniques are used by some of the most inspirational public speakers and influential presenters in the world.

Why does storytelling for presentations work?

When you hear a story, your brain is put to work. Your brain responds as if it were a real experience. Think about the last time you watched a horror film, were you scared? Think about the last time you read a sad novel, did you cry? This is the reason that stories hold our attention so well, for our brain, the story is processed as if it were happening to us. We are completely and utterly absorbed.

Harnessing the power of storytelling for presentations

So, for the best presentation, all you need to do is tell a story. Easy? Storytelling is an extremely powerful communication tool and harnessing that power can transform your presentations, but chances are you might need a few tips and techniques to help you get the most out of storytelling.

Here are our top 5 storytelling techniques to help you ace your next presentation:

1. Choose the right story

Make sure the story you choose is relevant to the point you want to make in your presentation.

Don't just throw a story into the mix just for the sake of it because we said it works. Your story needs to appeal to your audience, to their needs, and their problems. It needs to be relatable. If you're not sure, ask yourself what am I trying to say?

2. Something needs to happen

For a story to captivate your audience something needs to happen, there needs to be some sort of conflict or action. In traditional stories, it's an evil villain that the character needs to defeat; in your presentation it might simply be a problem or struggle that your character needs to overcome.

3. Create drama & suspense

Every good story needs a beginning middle and end. That's what you were taught in school right? Well, it's not necessarily true. Sometimes, a resolution isn't always needed to make a story complete. Leaving your audience hanging can create suspense & drama. It can be especially useful when you're trying to illustrate a point in a presentation too.

4. Get personal

Don't be afraid to be human and show emotion. By getting personal, you open yourself up to your audience. This can make you feel vulnerable but it will allow your audience to feel empathy and understand where you're coming from and this can be hugely persuasive.

Business Storytelling Tips to Guide Your Next Presentation

Who doesn't enjoy a good story? Storytelling is a natural form of communication that is used in every culture. It is an age-old tradition passed down for generations to help others understand backgrounds, beliefs, and experiences. A good story engages various parts of the brain and draws people in, grabbing their emotions, evoking empathy with the characters, and allowing them to visualize the story elements. Listeners stay tuned wanting to know more about the journey unfolding, keeping their attention engaged and imaginations active.

Many scientists believe that humans are hardwired for storytelling. Neuroscientist Uri Hasson of Princeton University is just one expert who has done research showing the effects of storytelling on the brain. Using functional magnetic resonance imaging (fMRI), Hasson and team scanned the brain activity of several participants while they listened to a story. Once the story began, the brain activity of the listeners synced up on a deep level, and "neural entrainment" spread across all brains in higher-order areas including the frontal cortex and the parietal cortex. This deep alignment did not happen during other tests in the study. For example, when the story recording was played backward, the brains showed some alignment of neural responses only in the auditory cortices.

Similarly, listening to random scrambled words from the story or entire sentences cited out of order also did not reach very deep in the brain. Even more surprising, the storyteller's brain activity was studied while telling the story and also synched with the listeners. Hasson concludes that an effective storyteller causes the neurons of an audience to closely sync with the storyteller's brain, which has significant implications for presenters.

Using storytelling as a tool in the business world is gaining lots of traction. However, despite studies on this topic showing how well-crafted stories can be more memorable and persuasive, the value of this art has not been completely accepted or practiced. So whether delivering training about a complex idea, proposing a solution to prospective customers, or presenting business plan for a new start-up, you'll want to brush up on your storytelling techniques.

To help deliver impactful stories during your next presentation, take a look at these useful tips. Also included are insights gathered from business storytelling professionals' websites that give more perspective on how to put the tips to work.

Understand your audience.

Knowing your audience's pain points and what they value and what they don't will help you tell the right story. Find out what topics interest your target audience or what other brands or people they trust. Try to determine if there are any shared experiences to highlight. Really understanding who you are talking to is a crucial first step in your storytelling journey. Nancy Duarte is the founder of Duarte, a firm that helps businesses realize the power of persuasive visual stories and presentations. In explaining how to identify your target audience, Nancy says, "Make sure you find common ground with the people to whom you're presenting. Common ground helps create empathy; if an audience can relate to the story you are telling them, they'll empathize with you and may begin to care."

Know Your Message

Be sure to understand what you are trying to convey to the audience and how your story relates to the action you want them to take. How do you want the audience to feel about your message? Of course, at some point in the sales cycle, your presentation needs to cover product features. And at some point at the annual kick-off meeting, stakeholders need to hear facts and figures. However, that information should be delivered in an interesting way to make it memorable. Mike Wittenstein founded Storyminers and views stories as a strategic business tool. In an interview blog he explains, "Instead of sharing stories about the numeric outcomes a leader hopes for, develop clear storylines that let people see and feel what the journey of getting to the goal will be like for them."

Ensure your story has a structure

Ensure your story has a structure. A story should include specific periods and names and relatable characters. And it needs to have a beginning (set-up), a middle (contrast or conflict), and an end (resolution and key takeaways). The contrast in the story creates drama. The current frustrations your audience faces can be contrasted with the bright future that's ahead. Consultant firm The Hoffman Agency has a business storytelling blog that sums it up nicely: "...the concept of contrast is one technique that always resonates with participants. The old way vs. the new way. Before vs. after. With vs. without. All deliver a form of contrast that resonates with the human brain."

Be authentic

Business storytelling should not be fictional. If the audience can relate to a real-life story, you are making a connection and building trust. And people like to do business with companies they trust. "Listeners sense authenticity, and if they don't see it, they will reject the story and the teller. The leader's rejected story will become fodder for the powerful 'water cooler' stories and will work against the leader's efforts," explains Molly Catron, an organizational consultant, storyteller, and keynote speaker who works with various businesses.

Use a conversational tone

Use a conversational tone and common words to help your audience relate to you as a person. You will come across friendly and put the audience at ease. Ian Sanders, a consultant, business storyteller, and author advises that stories should be kept simple. You should speak to the business audience as if you are speaking to your friends or family. You do not need to look through a thesaurus just because you're presenting in a business context.

Remember the audience is the hero

The product should not be the hero and neither should the presenter. Your audience should be able to see themselves as the hero in your story. Can they relate to the experience you're telling? The Buzz Factory's Gail Kent talks about how important it is for businesses to tell stories through great content. But, the business needs to act like the mentor and allow the customer to see himself in the story as the hero.

Make human and emotional connections.

Like visuals, emotions also enhance retention. On top of that, research by neuroscientist Antonio Damasio shows that emotions play a vital part in decision-making. His findings have big implications for presenters who are trying to persuade audiences to take action. Doug Stevenson is the founder and president of Story Theater International, a speaking, training, and consulting company that delivers corporate storytelling advice. In one of his keynote speeches Doug explains, "Speak from your head, deliver your content, deliver the message that you know you have to deliver, but keep your heart wide open so that they feel who you are...they have to feel that while you deliver your content." Be approachable, craft a connection aligned to your brand, and think about what you want the audience to feel.

Best Storytelling Tips for Marketing Presentations

What's the worst horror story you can imagine for

Presenter giving a marketing presentation? She is falling in love with his or her story!

Recently, I coached a presenter. He was 'all over' stories. And truthfully, his storytelling ability was great if you wanted to sit around the campfire for hours and hours on end.

But, for a business setting, his commitment to storytelling was a death sentence. During his presentation, I looked around the room. People were staring at the ceiling. Others were examining their watches as if they contained hidden gold. No one wanted to hear one more colorful word — not one more elaborate metaphoric example.

Know what I'm talking about? It's the storyteller syndrome. It is gone overboard.

In every part of presenting, there is a risk. You can take a good thing and drag it into the ground by overdoing it.

This does not have to happen. Use these three tips to make sure you use storytelling to your advantage in marketing presentations.

Tip 1: Stick to the Point

In business presentations, unlike campfire stories, you have to stick to the point. Many audiences are filled with people who are already overloaded and overwhelmed with information.

If you want to keep their attention, you must stick to the point. Watch out for any tendency to drift off topic with your favorite colorful examples.

Hint: if this is a problem for you, work with a colleague. If they notice you are going off track, establish a hand signal to mark the moment. Then, be sure to use this signal to refocus your message and stay on point.

Tip 2: Read Your Audience

Read your audience the same way you read the gauges in your car. Are you running on empty? Does your audience need a bio-break? Are they getting fidgety and restless? Are people edging to the door or fixating on their watches?

Watch for the signs and symptoms of disengagement. If you notice these, switch to a more focused delivery style.

You can win your audiences' attention if you keep their signals at the forefront of your awareness.

Tip 3: Let Your Audience Speak

Storytelling is not a one-sided activity. Ask questions. Get people talking. Use their comments and questions to infuse energy and creative spark into your story.

Nothing is as exciting as spontaneous interaction. When you use this in your storytelling, you will not be at risk of talking to a bored or restless audience.

In addition to participants having a chance to speak, other people in the audience often connect with comments made by peers. These comments provoke interaction, discussion, and collaboration.

Professional presenters often use storytelling to express ideas, emphasize key points, and engage audiences. With persuasive storytelling, you can inspire creativity and collaboration.

Effective storytelling is the mark of a distinguished leader and presenter. If you want to connect with your audiences, get familiar with planning, preparing and performing with stories.

As one of my clients puts it: "you get better results with better planning." This is a smart business and a smart storytelling practice.

Develop your business storytelling skills so you can communicate effectively to your audience. Persuasive visual stories can help you reach more customers and grow your business.

The Benefits of Good Presentation Storytelling

There are a lot of tips and techniques you can take advantage of to make a killer presentation. You can come up with valuable content, share interesting data, and make beautiful infographics. Nothing will engage your audience and drive it to action more than a compelling story. This part of this book will explore the benefits of good presentation storytelling that needs to shine in your deck.

Storytelling Creates an Immersive Experience

There are a few reasons that presentation storytelling makes such a major impact. One big reason is that a good narrative will tap into the emotions of your audience and allow them to relate and empathize with the message you're trying to convey much more than facts and figures alone.

That's because, according to the New York Times, when we're told stories, our brains often don't differentiate fact from fiction; instead, we tend to immerse ourselves in the stories as though we're part of them. This, in turn, makes it easier for us to connect to any given idea and empathize with both the message and the person telling the story.

Storytelling Inspires Audiences to Take Action

Humans tend to be driven by their emotions. According to Jane Praeger, a strategic storytelling professor at

Columbia University's Strategic Communications and Communications Practice program, "[We] like to believe we are logical, but we use data and facts to post-rationalize the decisions our emotions have already driven us to make."

Therefore, using a strong narrative to tap into the emotions of your audience is a great technique for compelling action. And it's one you can use in any presentation, no matter how dry the data or content is that you're sharing.

Let's say you're presenting about a new product. Rather than focus solely on its features and capacities, walk your audience through how the product came to be. Discuss any setbacks, trials and tribulations, and the defining moments. This will allow your audience to feel more connected to the product and increase their desire to buy it.

Storytelling Makes Your Presentation More Memorable

You can put hour after hour into your preparations, but if no one remembers what you present, all of that time and effort is for nothing. This is where presentation storytelling can step in to help.

Weaving a narrative into your deck is one of the most effective presentation techniques. Ensure your time doesn't go to waste and that your audience remembers your message. In fact, according to Jennifer Aaker, a professor at the Stanford Graduate School of Business, "stories are remembered up to 22 times more than facts alone."

Think about it this way: let's say you watched two presentations about the benefits of meditation.

The first presentation shared health statistics, an analysis of what happens to the brain before and after meditating, and improvements one can hope to gain after practicing it.

The second presentation includes the same information. But the presenter gave a personal account of how their depression made them question whether they wanted to live at all. Meditation changed that completely.

Which one are you more inclined to remember? Of course, it's the one with the compelling story behind it.

Now that you know the benefits of good storytelling, are you ready to elevate your presentation game to the next, next level? Then check o ut this presentation training we've designed to help you do just that.

CHAPTER 3: STORYTELLING FOR BUSINESS PURPOSES

Stories and Storytelling are Good for Business

What do you think of when you hear the term "storytelling"? If you're like most people, your mind may wander through several common scenarios. You may think of a father telling his child a goodnight story. You might remember evenings around the campfires of a camp swapping ghost stories. You might think about those who bring history to life with tales of their long-past younger years. There are so many different possibilities. If you're like most people, though, you'll probably overlook one of the most powerful uses for storytelling. Storytelling for business is growing in popularity and is widely recognized as a powerful communication supplement.

The idea is relatively simple. We all know that narrative structures engage people in very personal and meaningful ways. There's nothing quite like a story to get an idea across. It's been those ways for centuries, and it continues to be true. From Aesop's fables to Zimbabwean tribal leaders, storytelling has had an impact. It's been used so long and so often for one very simple reason: it works like a charm.

Stories connect with us. They interest us. They get our attention. They appeal to our creative instincts, our analytical tendencies, and our creative minds. They do things that "just the facts" approaches can't even come close to rivaling. Storytelling for business merely recognizes that potential and finds an application for it in the professional realm.

That doesn't mean preceding other, more traditional ways of communicating to focus on telling tall tales. Effective storytelling for business requires a bit more subtlety than that. Successful use of narratives in business involves utilizing them to underline key points and to communicate important ideas with an extra level of persuasiveness. Effective storytelling for business can take many different forms, but it's rarely as simple as telling an anecdote to those assembled for a board meeting.

How do we convince the business world that a good story holds more power and is more memorable than hearing and/or reading a descriptive paragraph that relates to an accomplishment, a procedure, a product, etc.? This became so evident recently when I was part of a committee judging nominations for the Regional Company and/or Organization with the Best IT (Information Technology) Training Program.

There were several criteria that we were to grade. The nominees had been asked to write a 250-word paragraph for each of the seven criteria. Most of the criteria were straightforward and asked for descriptions. I could hardly wait, however, until we reached the final one: "Do you have any great Success stories?"

You can imagine my disappointment to find that only one of the nine nominees told us a story. The others blabbed on about profits and accomplishments, etc. The one with a true and moving story -- about a young man who was helped by the training to get a job and a scholarship that turned his life around -- won our vote. The sad part is that I know that every one of the companies or organizations has plenty of success stories. They just don't know how to tell them. What is the solution?

First, don't call it "storytelling." Even though publications all over the nation -- and even the world -- are writing about the companies, organizations, and trainers who are making use of the power of storytelling, very few of the upper echelon will react well to our telling them that they need "storytelling." So many people have the wrong perception of what storytelling entails. They think it is a quaint event that is performed for children in schools or the local libraries.

We can tell them that the World Bank now uses storytelling for information sharing and that a company called EduTech produces a publication called ASK for NASA that consists of employee stories. Todd Post, the editor, writes, "The success we've had with it (ASK) has allowed us to examine our problems holding onto knowledge. Right there in front of our noses was a successful model to emulate." They then created What You Know, which is EduTech's storytelling magazine.

We have to use all of our imagination to work storytelling into meetings, marketing, and everyday encounters. We all know that the stories are there. I suggest taking a small notebook to work or to a company you know well (you may do some freelance work for them or know others who do) and start writing down the casual stories you hear at the water fountain, on the way to an appointment, at lunchtime and in the elevator. Start asking those who had worked a long time at the company/organization about history -- how it was when they were hired and why they have stayed there. When awards are presented, interview those who receive them -- get the full story.

What great success stories does your business have? Start making use of their power, and you will be amazed by how quickly the word travels.

If you aren't using storytelling to your advantage, it's time to broaden your communicative horizons. By learning the art of bringing the narrative to the workplace, you can improve the key points of communication and persuasion. With a little guidance and instruction, you can make one of humanity's most powerful means of forging persuasive connections a regular part of your business life.

DANIEL ANDERSON

The Incredible Art of Storytelling in Branding

Stories came into existence as a human life came into existence. When language was not even invented, or linguistic skills are not acquired, humans conveyed stories through different forms such as carvings, symbols, or paintings. The caves and temples are proof that humans told stories since their existence. Human lives have been reflected in those stories, and people resonate themselves through those stories. Then languages were developed, and other forms of storytelling were invented. From dance forms to writing novels, stories have been told through every possible medium. Humans are more responsive to stories than facts. Businesses need to keep this in mind and devise branding strategies to associate with customers.

The inclusion of storytelling to reach customers has a lot of benefits. The stories about how the business was started, what it stands for, and what change it has made or how it impacted people's lives should be told. There is no end to stories and experiences about any product or service or development process of those products. People relate to stories and stories told based on the theme or purpose of business will resonate with people and it will help in gaining a loyal customer base. This is why Apple has become one of the most valuable brands in the world and has millions of loyal customers. When a new product is launched, people want to use it. Though there are better or advanced products available at lower prices in the market, people want Apple gadgets only. This is because of the story Apple tells about thinking different, staying hungry & staying foolish, and many more. From its foundation in the garage of Steve Jobs to become.

- Multi-billion dollar company, it tells stories, and it does not only sell products but gain loyal customers.

Another important aspect of storytelling is being honest. People can detect lie, and any fabricated story will make a negative impression of a brand. Every business is unique and has a unique story behind it. The individuality must be determined and conveyed through stories. Every person sees the world in their way, but the honest stories touch everyone's heart and help in connective with a brand. The honest expression of a story touches people and elicits a positive response. Moreover, honest stories stand apart from the crowd. This individuality is good for business and branding.

The flow and structure of a story need to be maintained to make people understand the message easily. The complicated structure and lack of flow will confuse people, and it will make negative impression. There must be a lot of ideation before telling a story and what should be included in the story. If there are elements that connect with people, the storytelling will be successful and favorable for business.

Being one of the leading branding companies in Pune and gaining wide experience in helping brands create awareness, Kaizen Design Studio helps businesses in telling stories in a creative manner that will help them in connecting with customers and creating a good market presence along with standing out from the competition.

STORYTELLING TECHNIQUES IN BUSINESS

Better Online Communication for Your Business

Once Upon a Time, there was a forward-thinking business that instead of bombarding their customers with facts, figures and sales content, they focused their time and attention on creating easily understood stories that customers could follow, understand and relate to.

As a concept, the method of storytelling within business makes perfect sense. We all know the basics of a story; the beginning, a middle and an end and importantly there isn't a single human on this earth that hasn't heard one. From our first ever steps on this planet we are brought up on stories.

Story will help us to understand a topic, relate to someone we've not met and help visualize a scene. The medium of storytelling is a great way to engage and maintain concentration levels while also reaching a more emotional, hard-wired part of the human brain.

With websites being the business mode of choice in the 21st Century it is important for businesses to make a good first impression. Another key area is to keep visitors on your site for as long as possible to maximize the chances of a sale, a quote or a contact. Instant statistics from any website are easily acquired; this includes user counts, users decisions/ actions, conversions, etc. Services such as

Google Analytics will give highly accurate data regarding any visitors.

The correct implementation of relevant and well thought out stories on your website is much more effective than the old style of information overload seen on many sales orientated websites. With the help of website analytics, the difference can be measured accurately.

Within the digital world, there are some great examples of the story in action. British Telecom's on-going tv advert storyline has created a decent following. BT allowed their followers to get in contact via social media and decide on the fate of the couple featured in the adverts. They had understood the huge benefit of storytelling marketing. Viewers can relate to the situations portrayed and also engage and affect the outcome.

The main aim of online marketing whether it takes the form of the story or the more outdated 'information dump' is to successfully communicate a message that will bring about some sort of behavior change or action as a result.

The storyline approach is best equipped to deliver the following:

1. Elucidate your message.

2. Explain why is Action Important.

3. Clearly define what Action is required.

4. What the Benefits and rewards will be.

When to Use Storytelling for Business

Storytelling for business is an interesting way to get an idea across. This strategy can be used in advertising campaigns, as well as to put a more human face on the company. Just like humans, a company has a history that suppliers and potential customers are interested in finding out more about.

When an advertising campaign includes a story, it immediately engages the reader or the person viewing it. They follow along and want to know what happens next. They can't help but think that the business using this technique is very creative and has something valuable to offer. Even when the product placement in the ad is at the very end of the story, the viewer or reader is likely to remember what it is and will want to learn more about it. That curiosity is what makes the story a good hook for bringing in new customers as well as making existing ones excited about what your company is doing.

Another way that you can incorporate a story into your business is on your company web site and other materials. Many visitors to the site will want to click on the "About Us" or "Our History" section of the web site to learn more about how the company was established. They will also be curious to find out more about how the business grew from its humble beginnings to the success it enjoys today.

Rather than put out a corporate face that is cold and

unfeeling, sharing information about the company and the people who work there makes it more approachable. If customers have the impression that their business is valuable to the company and that their questions and concerns will be listened to and addressed appropriately, they are more likely to come back for their future needs. Tell them about the company's philosophy, the good it's doing in the community or other information that will help the customer feel comfortable.

There are many ways that storytelling for business can help to improve your company's corporate reputation. Using this technique will make it more appealing to customers. You will also notice the difference in your business's bottom line.

Storytelling for Business - Getting Your Point Across

In business, one of the most important factors in success is making a personal connection with those you are working with. Whether you are connecting with customers, associates, or co-workers, storytelling for business can be an important tool in getting goals accomplished. Many think of storytelling as something that is best left for the children's bedtime, but in reality, good story can have a serious impact on the business world.

Many companies use stories to communicate their vision and roots to customers and clients. By telling a tale of a top-level executive within the company who struggled with adversity and rose to the top of the corporate ladder, they can project hope, drive, and determination. Those who are on that same level can connect with the adversity in the tale and want to contribute to their continued success.

Stories can also be a great motivator in the business world. This is why many companies hire motivational speakers to come into their conferences and meetings to inspire their employees. These people are master storytellers who have rehearsed their tales of finding the ambition to get the job done and done right. Other executives have learned the art themselves, becoming the source of inspiration for their team of workers.

Storytelling can also help within daily relations with

customers and coworkers. Because storytellers can draw people in and connect with them through their tales, these people make great supervisors or salespeople. These personal connections are what causes people to gravitate to them and listen to what they have to say. They can persuade a customer to buy or an employee to become more engaged in their work, with just a well-placed story.

Once you see how storytelling in business can have a direct impact on success, productivity, and profitability, you will likely begin to look for ways to incorporate it into your daily business practices. Spoken words can be extremely powerful, giving life to new ideas and allowing you to make a one on one connection with others. Once you have learned to be a good storyteller, you have the keys to success in the palm of your hand.

Effective Marketing through Story Telling

Many years ago, when I was just a young rookie salesman, I was fortunate to fall under the sway of a wonderful veteran sales manager. His name was Milton Lupow, and he became a mentor, teacher, and coach as I struggled to climb the ladder to success. The lessons he taught stick closely to me until this day and at every opportunity I introduce Mr. Lupow's concepts to my clients. When I became a sales manager, then an executive and business owner I appreciated his imparted wisdom even more.

One of the most important, and profitable lessons taught me by Milton Lupow was to sell by telling stories. Ben Franklin closes, take away closes, sales tapes and courses were the rages of the day in the marketing and sales world of that time. Hard selling was common. Mr. Lupow would have none of the trendy techniques.

His sales presentations were seminars in weaving product's features and benefits, and thus importance to the buyer and their customers, through placing the product in the center of a story. After many successful presentations, as we reviewed the meeting notes, we would discuss the customer's reactions. I began to notice that buyers enjoyed and looked forward to Mr. Lupow's visits as they were not the normal sales blather that was served up by competitors.

Product comparisons, figures, data points, market share and so many other important elements key to marketing and selling consumer products usually do not sufficiently differentiate your product from the competition. Telling stories does. Very few people enjoy being sold something. Everyone enjoys hearing a good story.

After 40 years in the consumer product sales, marketing and product development business I have enough experience to tell stories based on my history. Those many years ago I did not have this chest of knowledge to dip into. I learned to take some element of the product, research and obtain unique elements of origin, geography, harvest, processing, rarity or availability and weave that bit into my story.

For instance, when I was presenting a fragrance I would highlight the unique, exotic essential oils we utilized, how weather affected their price and access and how the flora or fauna that rendered the oils was discovered. Ambergris is collected from the surface of the ocean after whales vomit. Berber women process rare argan oil from endangered trees in the Sahara desert. Many ingredients are harvested in the Amazon by indigenous tribes. A kind of travelogue with cultural highlights frames the provenance of the product as I regularly called on customers I discovered, much as I had experienced with Milton Lupow, that the stories were successful in conveying a more positive image of my offerings also found out that I was more welcome each time I returned.

When I marketed pet products, the story might highlight how I had stumbled onto the product concept while watching dogs interact on the beach, or at a park, or my sister's pool party. I invented a wellness pet product by utilizing an ingredient I had found being used in medical surgeries. I had taken a quart of the compound and when placed in sealed, soft-sided bag pets love d to relax on the cooling unit. I discovered this by accident while relaxing at the beach.

If I want to convey how products can jump categories I might tell the story of the famous over-the-counter topical treatment Preparation

The product was developed by a Dr. Sperti, a Cincinnati-based chemist. It successfully provided hemorrhoid relief for generations. Some enterprising hemorrhoid sufferers somehow discovered that the properties that made the cream so effective in its targeted treatment also made Preparation H a terrific facial wrinkle cream. It became the base for some of the earliest wrinkle creams. That is a real leap.

Several years ago I worked on a gourmet food project. The product was wonderful. But it needed a better story to differentiate it from the competition. We perused the ingredients in the recipe and researched their supply sources. Targeting two key components of the label statement we developed a unique process story about them. We then bought minimum quantities of the ingredients from the most exotic, artesian sources and added them to the product. We now had a unique, rare, quality-driven story about the products special features and benefits versus the competition.

Process stories are excellent tools to utilize for cosmetic, aromatherapy, bath and body, wellness, food, drink, and other consumable products. A proprietary style of production that can be detailed, utilizing a unique engineering or lab process can be a huge difference maker. Ingredient stories alone are rarely enough to achieve success. A trade secret, highly specific method of handling, blending and producing is much more compelling and intriguing to buyers.

Learn to weave interesting stories and points of discovery into your product marketing and sales presentations. Your trade show meetings and sales appointments will be much more interesting and memorable. You will enjoy the increased sales too!

How Stories Can Rocket Your Profits

One of the many benefits of using storytelling in business is that it can communicate powerful messages about you and your product. In today's ever-changing and competitive market, using just facts to send out your important messages wouldn't cut it anymore.

People are looking for that something more that can move and inspire them, something that they can relate to. This is where the benefits of storytelling in business come in.

Since the beginning of time, stories have been used to share information, ideas, history, and knowledge. What makes them work is that they connect with people's feelings.

Humans are not always rational beings. Most of the time, they make decisions based on their emotions. It's important that you understand how you can use this to your advantage.

Stories Simplify the Complex.

Bombarding your potential customers with too much info is useless. After a while, they just tune out whatever it is you're saying, and your words get ignored.

It is important to understand that they will most likely trust someone they can understand. Instead of all these mere facts, tell a story about how and why these can be relevant to them. Not only will it save you time and effort, but it will also leave a good impression on your prospects.

Stories Produce Mental Images.

Facts and figures will be immaterial if they are not able to make an impact. By slipping in all this information in a story and setting your customers' imagination in motion, you can create a strong mental image.

The role of storytelling in business is that it forms the visua l ima gery that he lps capture ideas and increases their ability to be understood.

Stories Help People Cope With Change.

Change is constant and inevitable. Most people dislike change, whether good or bad. Amend this impression by using a story conveying that change doesn't necessarily mean disaster and loss.

An effective way of using storytelling in business is by addressing the customers' fear, uncertainties, confusion or anger through a story that they can relate to. This will help them understand the situation better and create a more positive outlook on it.

By using storytelling in business, you get more of your messages across to your customers. Make yourself memorable to them by being clear and simple. Having a sense of humor can be a bonus too. Don't rely on the facts too much. Remember, the key is to connect!

Storytelling Techniques for Marketing Online

Everyone's heard the storytelling secrets, "Facts tell; stories sell"...

Unfortunately, when I first marketed online, I felt that I didn't have a personal story wo rth sharing, so I used the "fake it tills you make it" technique.

And hence, this is the problem with online marketing today. We all start from somewhere, and if we all try to fake when we start - then who can anyone ever trust online?

But be me?

They say that storytelling in business on video is the fastest way to success, but the idea of getting in front of a camera and telling my story was scary!

Clicked "exclude this page" on my "about me" page on my first blog that I ever created online because I was shy about coming out with my real story. Now that's part of my story when I make my videos thought, "Why would anyone want to know more about me?"

After blogging for a few years, I found out the hard way that people are interested in hearing stories about other people - both good and bad. And, even if you don't have a "success story" that you believe people would be interested in, there is always some achievement to be found.

You can talk about how you got your first free lead online or how you screwed up your auto-responder and wasted your first 100 leads before learning - but now others can learn from your mistakes.

When you're telling true to life stories in video form, people who follow you get to feel that they know you. And, you know what they say, "people will buy from people who they know, like and trust"... and that's YOU once you can establish an emotional connection!

"That can't be all there is," you're saying... "What are the REAL storytelling secrets?"

OK, here are some storytelling tips to get you started...

Determine who you want to influence.

In other words, determine your target market. Try to imagine what kind of person you might be talking to - you know, the kind of person that's going to Google right now and typing in your keyword phrase. Try to figure out exactly what this person is looking for.

Determine why you want to influence this type of person.

If find it's easiest to image a single person going to Google and looking for a solution to their problem. I just speak as though I have that solution. Once you do it some times, your speech becomes more confident, and it's not long before you're presenting yourself as a leader.

This person in your imagination has a problem. Identify with their problem but telling a similar story about yourself or someone you know. Be sure to elicit emotion by telling your personal story.

Example: "I remember when I first tried to figure out my auto-responder, and I was so lost I didn't even know what questions to ask to get help"...

Determine what it is that you want them to do.

This is where you "bridge" people while keeping them engaged emotionally. Telling a story of how you or someone you know was in this hopeless state with this particular problem, and you found the solution to this problem by watching the same video that they now have access to, etc.

People only want to know that there's hope for them, too. When you can make that emotional connection provide that hope - you just made a new online "friend."

It is a fact that even logical people buy based on emotion. When people listen to you or read your story, they put themselves in the story and connect emotionally.

Storytelling For Internet Marketers

We live in the "Cyberspace Era" where attention span has dropped dramatically. Even those of us who used to loll in a comfy armchair reading a book are finding we can't concentrate for so long.

Have you noticed how you have become a nervous clicker when you are on your computer? Own up. Do you read long articles online? Or do you do what most Internet surfers do, which is to quickly scan, forefinger poised to click through to the next page or website?

If you are in the Internet marketing business, you know you have to get your message across fast.

There is still a place for good storytelling. Our attention spans may be shortening, but we still enjoy a good tale - especially if it appeals to our emotions, our struggles, and our pains.

So if you are trying to make money online, it is good to keep in mind that stories - even very short ones - can help to engage your potential customer or lead.

So much sales copy is bland or over-hyped and relies on popular keywords in an attempt to rank high. It is hard to get around this. But there are opportunities to inject an element of storytelling that might interest your potential customer.

Very often people want to read of somebody like themselves who has struggled and has finally found success. Sure, the rags-to-riches stories have been over-played, but such storytelling resonates have found good storytelling can captivate an audience. As a journalist, I have transitioned from the old school forms of journalism to the modern online copy. I've had news and features stories published that were 3,000 to 5,000 words in length. I've had the chance to include action, anecdote, and description to grab the reader by the throat and pull them through the story right until the end.

Today, as an Internet marketer and a journalist, it is unlikely that I will write a story or article that is longer than 700 words. And much of my marketing focus on short, sharp adverts that have to grab the potential customer and get them to click through to read the sales copy or watch a video with the hope they sign up or make a purchase.

But even in this process, storytelling can help - even in the short text ads that are so common nowadays.

If you are selling your product, or even if you are selling somebody else's product as an affiliate, you may be able to inject some personality or story into your ad and sales copy. Maybe it is a brief mention of your own story or that of the makers of the product you are selling.

Potential customers need something to relate to. You have to appeal to their emotions. You have to offer them the dream.

You've probably seen this before:

- School drop-out becomes a millionaire

- How I went from debt to riches

- Losing 30 pounds led to success with the girls

- I used to wait tables; now I am a millionaire

- I used to be shy; now I speak publicly to thousands.

Maybe you have a chance in your landing page and in the sales copy for a short story to be told - your story or that of the creator of the product you are selling. Done well, it can help appeal to the emotions of your potential buyer. But it can be tricky because you may be trying to stuff your advert with relevant keywords. You will have to consider what is the right balance between keywords and story.

If there is a story to be told, try to use it.

Unbreakable Rules for Storytelling in Email Marketing

How are you telling your business story? Most often email marketing is a core part of how you are presenting your brand and business to customers and prospects.

This week, I got a remarkable email. Sounds funny, right? The reason it was remarkable was this: it was a story that got me to take action.

Don't know about you, but I get a lot of emails. Sometimes over 200 a day. So, when I saw a good story - it made me stop and think. How did they do it? I've found that there are three unbreakable rules for telling marketing stories in an email.

The nuts and bolts of storytelling are simple enough - but it's necessary to understand the mind-set of your customers and clients. Are they strapped to a desk - bored out of their minds? Are they inundated with tons of emails in a cluttered in-box? Are they distracted by personal obligations and family problems pulling on their attention?

Even without knowing you or your clients, there are a lot of business, family, personal and social demands for attention. And you can bet there are a lot of things on almost everyone's mind.

So, the big question in storytelling for email marketing is this:

Why should anyone pay attention to you?

I know it seems a bit harsh. But you must answer this question...if you want to tell a compelling story and make your email stand out.

Let's look at the 3 Unbreakable Rules right now.

Rule 1: Grab Attention In The Headline

Even if you have a terrific story - you have to get people to open your email. The subject line is the single most important part of your presentation when it comes to email.

This is very similar to headlines, magazine covers, and book covers. Sure, you must have something interesting to say inside. But the headline is what pulls people in.

If you want your busy clients to read your story, work on your subject line! Many experts in writing advise spending 90% of your time on the headline. The same kind of targeted focus on subject lines is a smart practice.

Rule 2: Stick To A Single Story

Nine times out of ten: tell a single story. Don't go wandering off in the woods and swamps of your lifetime full of experience. Stick to your story. Avoid adding fancy frills and twists. Stick to your story.

Tell a single story, and make sure it's one that matters to your reader. Do this, and you're going to get a better response...even in an overloaded brain.

Hint: a single story is simple your emails short, and you're surprise. People are much more and short. Keep in for a pleasant likely to respond!

Rule 3: Focus on A Single Action

Yes, it's tempting. Maybe you've got several actions you want your busy client to take. Do not be swayed. Stick to ONE single action.

If you give people several actions to take, what will happen? A big nothing. Too many choices may be your worst enemy.

Instead, keep things simple. One. What could be simpler than that?

Information is a double-edged sword. On the one hand, it can be used to share valuable insights with people across boundaries, across economic barriers, and across time. On the other hand, it can paralyze people into non-action.

But now you know. You know how to focus your emails and inspire people to take decisive action.

Let's just recap:

- Create a compelling subject line.

- Tell a simple story.

- Provide a single action to take.

Not too rough, eh?

Develop your storytelling skills and win results. Tell persuasive stories in email marketing and face-to-face presenting. Discover how to reach more customers, stand out in a crowd, and grow your business.

DANIEL ANDERSON

Storytelling in Marketing: Engaging Your Customers in the Brand's Journey

Storytelling seems to be the ultimate weapon these years in the world of Marketing. At a time when in-bound Marketing is the keyword of every best practices publication, connection with your customers on a direct and ongoing communication basis has jumped from the nice-to-have assets to the must-haves.

What this conveniently broad word is all about, is blend of immersion and integration: catch the consumers' interest through narratives; make them discover your philosophy and what you stand for through simple messages, and drive them into your brand's history by making them a part of your moves.

One company that got that right over the past years is a leading beverage company that you all know for its sparkling brown soda, and that is already so familiar to every one of us that you would think it doesn't need to invest in communication anymore. WRONG. It remains familiar by regularly talking to its customers and making them act. The marketing team in that company proved it again lately by launching two highly imaginative campaigns focused on interaction with their customers. One of them featured a food truck traveling around the globe, spontaneously drawing customers to stop by and eat together, creating the whole experience by themselves. More recently, the other campaign had participants try to make it to the 6th platform of a crowded train station in 70 seconds, in a James Bond-like race against time, to win tickets for the premiere of the movie Skyfall. Lately, the company launched yet another campaign, printing hundreds of first names on its canned drinks, inviting customers to "share it with..." a person they like.

So what is it that such a massive brand specifically wants to use storytelling for?

First of all, it connects your people and the people you target your strategy. No more vague positioning such as "make it matter" or "make it happen" that confuses even the company's employees, no more one-way messages separating the brand's offering and the customers' expectations.

It improves the efficiency of your communication efforts because people seem to retain information better when presented in the form of a story. Stories and unexpected/uncommon experience with a brand also help to generate buzz marketing and let the story spread massively through your target on its initiative, without you having to spend a dollar on a referral system!

It gives you control over the story of your company and what you stand for: you don't want the customers to build their picture of who you are and risk to miss what's most important about your business, or not make up their mind at all and forget all about your message right away.

And at the bottom line: it helps to significantly increase the dollar value of your products and your brand. A study conducted on over 100 products sold on eBay showed that even at a micro level, stories could increase product value by more than 25 times its original price. Tiffany & Co gained 10% stock value after launching their "What makes love true" brand story. Burberry's stock price increased by 750% since it actively implemented storytelling in its marketing in 2008, through video content and social media.

Three keys to effective Storytelling

To reap the benefit of successful story-based marketing, you have to make it right. Marketers must think like publishers in the way they bring content to their audience and communicate with it. There are several keys to effective storytelling:

Authenticity: In the message conveying the brand's philosophy and values. It establishes the credibility of the company vis-à-vis consumers. Without credibility, the best stories are mere lies that can only drag people away from you;

Content: Words, images, sounds, form, characters that resonate with people, through the use of quality and emotional components, mixed with rational elements;

Value added: The search for a reward like in the campaign using James Bond, or entertainment for the watchers. The question to answer is "what's in there for the customer?"

Implementing a story into the brand's communication or product offering may use various ways: from an original and meaningful packaging, like the perfume Paper Passion by Steidl, whose box is actually a book, to retrospective videos such as the LEGO story and bottled whisky brand Johnnie Walker's "keep walking" advertising, both telling the history of the companies with a visual-friendly graphic style or half-humorous tone.

How to Use Storytelling for Business and Why It Matters

Every great speaker is a great storyteller. Why? Because the audience can retain information BETTER when people can emotionally and viscerally connect to what's being said. If you think back to childhood, stories were - for many of us - an introduction to life 's lessons, to human behavior, morals, ethics and right versus wrong. And we remember still the value of those stories and what they taught us, not to mention the vivid imagery they conjure up.

The use of storytelling in business is growing and for a good reason. As the necessity of communicating the value and benefit of what you do to the world increases, the skill with which you articulate that, requires some imagination and uniqueness to capture the audience's attention... and keep it. By activating the imagination of the audience through stories, you, as the speaker, engage the audience to participate in an experience that is both captivating and informative. It's a perfect way to connect to the content of your message. The emotional thread of story is a direct line to the brain for memory retention and the processing of information. In a sense, you are providing an effortless way to learn using a technique that has been instilled in us since childhood.

Here are some great ways to weave a story into your speech or interview:

- Be brief. A story should have a strong beginning, a

colorful, clear middle, and a great ending. And if the story is within a speech, make it 6-8 sentences. You dissipate the impact of a story if it rambles on too long or is too repetitive. Choose your words wisely and make them count!

- Paint a picture of a great central character and take us to a different time and place. Set it up well and describe it with a few, choice descriptors. Add a bit of dialogue in the character's vernacular. It will make the character come to life.

- Know WHY you are telling this story. What is the point of your story and how, very specifically, does it tie into your talking points. Make sure you have the connector! And weave it in seamlessly.

- Use some dynamic and inflection in your voice when you tell a story. Incorporate some pacing - don't rush. Be a little theatrical (little being the operative word) and let us relish the tale.

And remember your story is NOT your bio. Put that in a document. Your story, any story you choose to use in your business communication should be told with humanity and wisdom, a bit of flair and with a take-away for your audience.

Storytelling for Business - The Surprising Benefits

When most people think of storytelling, images of toddlers cuddled in bed and ready to drift off to sleep spring to mind. While at its most basic, this is precisely what storytelling is, the principles of storytelling can have surprising applications in the real world. Storytelling for business allows messages to be presented in a way that is easy to understand and appealing for a variety of audiences.

Stories allow complex ideas to be broken down into easy to understand terms. Consider the most prominent religious figures throughout the world. Nearly all of them were storytellers on some level. Their talent for drawing in their audience and captivating them into believing that everything they spoke was true and important was what made them into the religious icons seen today. Businesses can harness this same power and draw in customers, or train their employees more effectively.

The personal connection felt between a storyteller, and their audience is what makes this art form so useful in businesses. Trust is a major factor in relationships, whether they are between employer and employee, business and customer, or between coworkers. Good storytellers will gain the respect and trust of those around them, improving their business relationships and making themselves more useful and profitable.

There are two main areas of business where storytelling

is the most effective. Stories are useful in customer relations and also in employee productivity training. These aspects of business provide one on one opportunities to connect with others and present important points to them. By finding ways to incorporate storytelling into these efforts, businesses stand a much higher chance of having their message heard.

Storytelling for business will only be effective if you have taken the time to learn just what it takes to be an effective storyteller. Having a grasp on public speaking will give you a solid advantage to put this powerful tool to use. Watch accomplished storytellers in action, then emulate the techniques you see. Once you have mastered this dying art, you can use it to drive business and to improve the performance of your organization's employees.

CHAPTER 4: HOW TO TELL STORIES TO YOUR OWN SUCCESS

Why You Should Tell Your Story

Why worry about your story? So often we tell the story of our business, but disregard the value of the ingredient of our personal story; it's your experience, your struggles and your subsequent successes that can create a real emotional connection to your potential clients or customers.

It is the connection that helps them to see that you are like them that you can understand where they are, and you are living proof that you have the solution to help them with their problem. Video and visual media can put you in the position to create rapport with your audience; your story can secure it, and move them closer to action (becoming a client, customer or even a sponsor).

Of course, we have more than one story, and other stories can be used throughout your marketing, interviews, and videos to create metaphors, highlight problems, and solutions.

The signature story though is one that can be used in visual media to create your following of enthusiastic fans (aka clients and customers).

Three secrets to telling your story with success?

- Don't disregard the best part; so often that thing that "no one will want to know" or that " you couldn't tell your customers" might be JUST the thing that helps your target market trust you. Idea: journal your most important moments in the development of your business, or career and share them with a trusted advisor or coach. You might be surprised at what will resonate with others.

- Focus on the recovery, not the problem; It's great to share your struggles and show where you've come from but keep the focus on your recovery and how it has helped you see clearly how to help others. Positivity is attractive and empowering.

- Be sure to have a few different versions; Have a short version, 30 seconds to two minutes, for networking and introductory videos. Plus, have a longer version that you can share in a longer format, like on stage or you're 'about us" page of your website. You may even do slight adjustments to emphasize different elements when you are speaking to a select niche audience.

Spend some time on your signature story. It may feel self-indulgent to some, but the ability to help others and increase your business is directly related to rapport with your market, and your unique story is the best way to connect that you've got!

Tell Your Story - People Want to Hear It!

Whether you are blogging for fun or a serious Internet marketer, you have a unique story. How you "tell your story" will separate you from everyone else.

Can you be real and truthful?

That depends on whether your story is real or truthful. You can't tell about your hugely successful Internet business unless it is. You can't talk about your world travels unless you have traveled around the world. If you do, you will eventually be "called out" by someone, and your secret will be exposed. Not something you will want to experience. Let that happen, and your story will never have any value!

You are telling your life story!

What if you don't have an interesting life story or a successful business career? No problem. You can write about someone else or what you would like to experience by visiting a particular place.

Let me give you an example.

"Frank Marino has been one of the most successful online marketers in recent times. He studied and learned video marketing and went from broke to a strong 5 figure monthly income in just a few months. His video marketing techniques have generated over 8000 leads during the past eight months. And he loves to share his unique process so that others can achieve success just like he did."

Frank's story is real and sounds better than mine, so it is to my advantage as an Internet marketer to highlight his life and accomplishments instead of mine. By telling his story, I add value to mine.

Tell your story about your travels!

What if you want to tell your story or a story about a visit to India. I have been there, but this would work whether I had or not. Check it out...

"Imagine seeing heaven for the first time. That's often the experience of many who visit the Taj Mahal in Agra, India. It's mesmerizing, and you can see the love that was put into the creation and then the construction of such a magnificent monument from a grieving man for the woman he loved. A must see in your everyone's lifetime."

By describing the situation and the reason for the building of the Taj, you create a real picture for your read er... one that is believable and worth taking the time to read.

Tell your story... truthfully!

Are you trying to become a powerful Internet marketing guru? Stop stealing space on Facebook timelines, email boxes or article directories with promises that you can't prove or justify. You will just become frustrated, and your audience will tire of your information. Become engaged with your audience. Learn about their needs. Provide solutions for their problems.

Start winning the battle today. Become one of the 3% who is successful online. As Dale Carnegie one said, "You ultimately get what you want when you help enough other people get what they want."

Spend some time deciding who you are. You were made to be special. You are unique. Invest in Yourself. You are worth it.

How to Pitch a Story

Ever wonder why we refer to convincing an editor

Story is worthy by "pitching a story?" I have. I'm a baseball enthusiast, and it makes a lot of sense to me. When the editor is at bat with you, he or she has a few swings to make before making a connection – through the story idea (ball) that could end up being a base hit or a home run. Naturally, everyone wants to hit a home run when they go to bat with an editor. Sometimes publicists and writers do have to walk to first base for the story assignment. Here are some helpful tips on how to pitch a story to an editor – and how to at least hit a single, double, or triple – if not a home run on occasion.

Use an Editor's Time Productively

Time spent on the telephone with an editor is more like a gift from God. If you want to be successful at purveying a story idea, it's best to have the information you want to convey rehearsed, or in note written form before your call. Try not to spend more than 10 or 15 minutes speaking about your story idea. Always ask the editor, "Is this a good time for you?" before beginning your pitch. Another great way to reach an editor is by a well-written e-mail pitch. In either case, focus the presentation or conversation on your story idea(s). If the editor is interested, he or she may ask more questions. If not, the editor should tell you.

Facts, Sources, Images

The editor needs to be interested in the theme of your story. A quick 2-3 sentence synopsis should offer an original focus or angle on a topic related to the publication. For example, if I wanted to pitch to Ms. magazine, I'd want to have a feminist event, profile, or feature idea that would be appropriate. Identify potential research sources for your story, or elaborate upon contacts with experts in the area, to let the editor know you are capable of tackling the subject. This expansion on your topic is key to keeping the editor's interest. Many magazine and newspaper editors will also ask you up front about the availability of photographs to go with the story. Be prepared to answer this question with some viable suggestions for photos and a creative approach. By now you've sold the story idea. So, don't forget to ask about the availability of a staff photographer from the publication to assist with photos.

Where do I Find Stories to Pitch?

Whether you are working for yourself or an organization or company, you have your comfort zones. These are vendors you are doing business with, your immediate environment, and social functions that seem aligned with your work. Go outside of your usual boundaries, an experiment in other social venues, and talk to people as often as possible. I look for story ideas when I'm on assignment with a story. Because I write daily, I know that one story will inevitably lead to another. I also pick up story ideas in the bar, at the university where I work as a teacher, from other clients, from students, local activists, or during outdoor group activities such as hiking and camping. I listen closely to what people say, and I carry around my favorite pocketbook sized bungee notebook to record my thoughts and story ideas. When I have an editor on the telephone or am lucky e nough to meet one in person, I act like I did when I played ball: I just start pitching.

Tools of the Trade

Once, I had a bead collection I acquired from a friend who was sick of beading. She said to me, "if you just look at the collection long enough, you'll have ideas." This is what I did, and this is how I made my necklaces.

For writers, I recommend they look at as many hard copies and online publications as possible. Don't forget to obtain a copy of the current Writers Market. It's a useful publication for profiling buying publications. I suggest the budding writer look into publications in sync with their interests. For example, I enjoy backcountry hiking and camping. I would probably want to contact outdoors magazines to pitch them some stories. I also have an interest in local newspapers, travel, educational, and holistic healing magazines. I've pitched to all of these types of publications. When you find a publication you like, write down the editor's name, e-mail, phone number and start to pitch. There's also a great writers' site called www.writingformoney.com. For $8 per month, you can review an interactive on-line listing of publications which are currently buying new work. With these links, you can visit the publications directly, read about them, and e-mail the editor your pitch. The longer you look at these tools of the trade, the more ideas will percolate.

Hit a Home Run

You want to hit a home run with an editor and land a story? Well, try going to bat with two to three story ideas instead of just one. Or the story you've developed can be pitched at different angles, which may make it more suitable for your publication of choice. Make sure to view at least several articles from the publication itself before pitching an editor so that you can have an idea of that editor's taste in material and style. All of these tips should help you land a great story, and even more in the future. As with baseball: practice. With practice, you'll learn how to pitch like an expert.

Using Your Story for a Stronger Audience Connection

How Stories Greatly Enhance Your Business Brand Positioning

Have you incorporated your story into your business marketing?

Recently attended a live event, WOW – Women of Worth, at Harrison Hot Springs where several women took the stage to inspire, educate and motivate the audience.

WOW, Event in Harrison Hot Springs 2016 Each of the guest speakers had their own unique story to tell, which captivated the audience and left us wanting to hear more.

What these women did so masterfully was incorporate their story into their presentation. By doing this, they quickly drew in the audience and built a strong "Know, Like and Trust factor" with them.

This immediately positioned them not only as experts in their field but also garnered the trust needed for the audience to take the next step and make a purchase.

And as a result, their "back of the room" sales exploded after their presentations.

Telling your unique story in your business will have your audience wanting more.

Stories Create Fascination

One of the memorable speakers was Leah Goldstein who spoke on Think Like A Champion: No Limits!

Leah infused her story of being a champion kickboxer, a Tour de France cyclist, a Race Across America Champion and the first female undercover sergeant in Israel and instructor of the elite Commando division.

Today she uses her story into her business where she's a motivational speaker and author and also offers wellness weekend workshops, personal and group training and nutritional planning.

How Leah uses her story to build her business compels people to work with her due to the fascination her story brings as well as the proof that she knows what she's talking about!

Stories Help Others Like You

KELITA is another speaker/entertainer who brought her story into her presentation. KELITA is a 5-time Juno nominee and multi-award-winning recording artist, songwriter, comedian, and inspirational speaker.

She had us in stitches laughing one minute and welling up with tears the next! Throughout her time on stage, she took the audience on a journey of her life.

Her story-telling approach had us all not just "Liking" her but LOVING her and wanting to support her; however, we could.

Stories Enhance Your Expertise

Brenda Eastwood brought a different kind of story to her presentation. Her story was based on her 30-year expertise as a nutritionist and how she changed women's lives when armed with the right knowledge about hormones.

By showcasing her expertise through her fact-based presentation plus sharing various success stories, the audience immediately trusted she knew what she was talking about and ran to her table to purchase her packet of recommended supplements.

Another incredible speaker was Olivia McIvor who talked about the Business of Kindness. Her story-infused presentation was similar to Brenda's where she brought the subject of kindness in the workplace to a scientific level, helping us all understand this is way beyond "WooWoo" stuff.

Her expertise was showcased as she brought her years experience in the HR field to her presentation filled with facts, figures and funny antidotes that taught us how to create a culture of kindness wherever we are.

Stories Create Loyal Followers

WOW Organizer Christine AwramEven the event organizer, Christine Awram brought her own story with her where she tragically lost her Mother just a few days before the event.

Her honesty, authenticity and genuine passion for the betterment of the women who attended ensured her not letting this personal tragedy affect their experience was not only awe-inspiring but truly admirable.

Do you think she will get loyal followers after this? You better believe it! Judging by how many women signed up for the April WOW event in Vernon (including me!) and even next year's event again at Harrison was a clear indication of the impact her story had.

Stories Will Build Your Business

Whether you are a speaker/presenter or not, there are plenty of opportunities for you to infuse your own story into your brand positioning for your business.

There are plenty of opportunities you can infuse your story into your business brand positioning story will help your audience connect with you on a level that no ad campaign can ever do. Give it a try the next time you write a blog article or write your about page on your website.

Methods on How To Tell Your Story So People Buy

As an entrepreneur, one of the most powerful weapons you have in your marketing arsenal is your own story. What do I mean by this? Well, on your website, your personal story should be crafted and conveyed in such a way that it appeals to your target consumers, allows them to relate to you and your business, and prompts them to take action and purchase your product or service. Remember, products don't sell themselves. It is up to you to convince consumers that your product and your business are worthy of their money, and a compelling story is one of how you can do this. How can you make the story that you're telling effective and engaging? Consider one of these storytelling models:

1. The Person-Driven Story:

This is the most common and what I use on my website's About Me page. In the person-driven story, sometimes also called a personal story, an entrepreneur will detail his or her journey to entrepreneurship. This will typically detail a painful, difficult, or challenging problem that an entrepreneur faced and then explain how the entrepreneur was able to conquer the challenge. There are some ways to maximize the appeal of this story. First and foremost, you want to make sure the challenge resonates with your target consumer. In other words, the symptoms, difficulties, or pain you experienced should closely mirror those that the target consumer is likely to be experiencing. For example, if you are selling a supplement to help combat male baldness, you will want to detail your experience with the problem - the insecurity it caused, the toll it took on your relationships, your lack of confidence, etc. If the target consumer can identify with the difficulties and challenges you faced, he or she is more likely to buy into your solution. This kind of story is all about facilitating an emotional connection between the entrepreneur and the target consumer.

2. The History-Driven Story:

The history-driven story is all about research. It will typically detail the history of a particular product or service. For example, imagine you are opening a massage parlor. You might detail the long history of massage, emphasizing its ancient origins and world-renowned healing properties. You then situate yourself and your business as the culminating moment of ever-evolving historic, ancient tradition. The idea is to make your product or servi ce sound exciting, relevant, and worthwhile using history.

3. The Guru-Driven Story:

Variant of the personal story, this focuses on a problem an entrepreneur faced and the "guru" that helped him or her to overcome the problem. Like in a personal story, you will want to focus on a painful, difficult, or challenging problem that you faced and the debilitating symptoms of this problem. However, in the guru-driven story, the entrepreneur doesn't come up with a solution to the problem. Rather, he or she turns to a guru for help, and the guru leads him or her along the path to a solution. Endowed with the wisdom and the insight of this guru, the entrepreneur is now here to help individuals who are facing the challenge that he or she once faced. This helps to boost credibility with the target audience, facilitating a connection.

Keep in mind that these three models are just suggestions. Whether or not you use one of these storytelling formats, keep in mind that a story that sells will always facilitate a connection with the target consumer. It's powerful connections that ultimately work to sell products.

Never underestimate the power of stories. If you need help crafting your story, apply for a Strategy Session so you can be on your way to selling more products/services.

How to Tell Your Story for Your Internet Marketing Business

As a business entrepreneur, one of the most effective ways to connect with prospective customers and team members is by integrating your personal story into your Internet marketing campaign. First timers, however, may find it difficult or intimidating to translate a personal story into words or video. I've developed six simple steps that will assist you in capturing an honest and truthful personal story.

Why do you need to tell your story as an Internet marketer? Simply put, because your story has the power to change someone else's life. Personal narratives give meanings and solutions to the fabric of our common existence. They connect us to our own lives and the lives of others. If told with simplicity and sincerity, a personal story can offer hope to those who find themselves in a similar situation.

One caveat: An embellished or exaggerated personal story may result in the adverse manipulation of the listener's actions or feelings. It can lead him or her to make inappropriate decisions, which will likely hurt them and will it detract from the messaging of your brand.

Therefore, it is crucial that when you incorporate your personal story into your internet marketing campaign, you stick to the truth. A story told with honesty and integrity is more likely to attract the right (read as "profitable") attention for your online business.

Here are six simple steps to transform your story into an effective Internet marketing campaign.

Write a short outline of the key points you want to elaborate on. Don't script it; rather, just jot down the most significant choices you made or actions you took on your entrepreneurial journey toward building an online business.

Sit with a friend and describe how your online business developed. Don't edit, don't judge yourself - just get the words onto a recorder. Any questions your friend asks can help you clarify why you felt the way you did or why you made certain decisions. Which of these had the most impact in determining your future as an online business owner?

Listen to your recording and note which elements most strongly touch the nerve of the inner processes that resulted in your outer successes.

Summarize your story on paper as a sequence of events. Define the situation (sometimes described as the "pain"), the search for an answer, the discovery of the solution, and finally the powerful diff erence it made in your life. This is the storyboard for your video.

Prepare to capture your personal story on video. An outdoor location is neutral and usually a soothing and non-distracting backdrop for the viewer. Be sure that you record in a well-lit area away from direct sunlight.

Transfer the video to digital format on your computer, and then edit the finished product. Don't try too hard to seem polished. Be authentic and be yourself-your personal story will resonate better with the viewer.

The best way to connect with your target audience is to relate the ups and downs of how you got into Internet marketing in the first place. Those who find themselves on a similar path will be grateful to you for your insight and expertise. Your brand is more likely to be fixed permanently within their minds as the result of an emotional connection.

Remember, the honest retelling of the sequence of events (situation-search-discovery-results) should occupy no more than 3 minutes of video. Don't be discouraged if it takes several attempts to capture it. Keep in mind that the more honestly your personal story is told, the easier it is to rehearse and the more compelling it will be to the listener. Have confidence in what you say, and it will resonate with potential clients.

How to Tell Your Business Story to Increase Your Sales

The elevator speech has as much mystery around it as a Hitchcock movie. It has been talked about and touted as the ultimate skill, so much so that it scares people to give it a go. Let me wipe out those fears and give you a formula for success.

You have probably been being a few uncomfortable situations where a person starts to explain what their business does, and after trying to pay attention to them for 7 minutes, you still have no idea what it is they do or if you would even need what they do. They probably talked about how they package their services or even their hourly rate; they may have even named dropped a few prominent people they have done work for. However, all of this doesn't give you the information you need to know if they can help you or they are just going to confuse you even more.

Sadly, this is far too common a problem with small business owners. They are trying so hard to grasp at anything that will give them credibility that they lose all credibility in their presentation. They are grasping because they don't have a firm grasp of what it is they do. They don't even understand themselves, and if they don't, they sure can't convey it to someone else in a logical and timely manner with confidence.

Let's look at the "elevator speech" and how to craft one that works. The key is in the questions that you ask yourself to reveal your true service and expertise.

What do you do?

What problem do you solve?

Who do you help?

How are you different?

Why is this important to me?

Let's look at the first question: What do you do? It seems basic enough; however, don't fill a page on what you do. Keep it short and to the point. For example, if you are a Realtor, you should state that you are an agent with XYZ. That is it, don't add any fluff this is not the place for it.

The next question is: What problem do you solve? Remember to keep it simple and "Twitter Size" your answer. So in the previous example, you might say, I help people find the perfect home for their needs.

The next question is usually a stumbling block because you have a fear of not being all-inclusive. The reality is no matter what service you offer it is not for everyone. If you have the best steaks in three states and I am a vegetarian, then you have excluded me. If you try to be all things to all people, you will be a master at helping no one. So in the same example, you might answer this buy saying I work with first time home buyers- or you might say you work with retirees looking to downsiz e. Whatever it is you need to focus on it and use it.

Let's examine the question: How are you different? What is it about you or your service that is unique? What separates you from the other people in your industry?

Maybe it is your speed of service or your personal touch. Whatever it is you need to identify it and own it. You might remember a small package delivery service that touted "when it positively has to be there overnight." If you continue with the example, it might be that you have the largest listing of houses in the XYZ school district.

Finally, you need to answer the question: Why is this important to me? Or you could ask why should I, the customer care? Many times business people ignore that what they think is important doesn't mean anything to the customer. This is how you connect with your customer. Get inside their head and find out what is important to them. What keeps them up at night? If we go back to our example, we might say that any new family needs to pay close attention to the school their children will attend.

So let's put our example together so you can see how it works.

Hello, my name is Jane Smith, and I am an agent with XYZ reality. I help first time home buyers find their ideal house. I have the largest listing in XYZ school district because you know how important it is for young families that their children attend the best schools in the area.

That is it. You don't need a diatribe you just need to convey a short message about yourself in a concise and confident manner. Now that you have it in writing you need to practice it until it rolls off the tongue. You may need to practice it times to get the feeling of confidence and connection, and once you do, you can face the world.

CHAPTER 5: A GUIDE FOR PERFECT STORYTELLING

The Power of Storytelling - How to Use It in the Business World

Every company and business has great stories. We need to hear them, tell them and internalize them. The biggest challenges, however, are convincing others of the power of storytelling and the impact it can have in the business world. How can we do this?

Start a small booklet of good company/ organization stories. Name the heroes and heroines. Ask others you trust to write up some stories for it. The stories should not be long, but all should include the beginning status quo, a character and characters, the crisis or challenge the climax and resolution, and how the original status quo was c hanged. Details are important, but should not be overwhelming.

With all of the easy-to-use desktop programs available today, you can put together a small booklet filled with these stories and give a copy to many of your peers. You will be surprised, once the word is out, how many other people will ask for a copy. It may be even time to start a small magazine or company newsletter that consists of stories.

Before a meeting starts (if you have any way of setting agenda items), ask if everyone would share a quick incident that they have recently encountered, what happened and if it changed their thinking and approach. Or ask what was the funniest happening last week. I know it may take some time to get this off the ground -- and, I don't suggest forcing everyone to take part in the beginning.

You will be amazed that if you can continue this quick story sharing introduction, those who haven't contributed before will start having a story to tell and everyone will look forward to this. I know a company that started adding half an hour to the end of their weekly sales meetings for a story sharing session. This soon became the most popular part of the meeting and, as storytellers know, the most valuable part of the meeting.

Once the storytelling starts to take hold -- and it will if you are persistent and keep it going -- the next step would be to call a group of the most enthusiastic story lovers and tellers together to work on the "Grand Narrative" of your company and organization. This will define what your group is all about. What describes the mission and goals in a clear and understandable way? It is OK to redefine your "Grand Narrative" even if you are a large, small, or even a one-person company.

Now is the time to take your storytelling plan to upper management. Convincing reasons that you can propose for capturing and using stories are to accomplish any of the following:

Share knowledge for succession planning. Promote team development to enhance productivity.

Exemplify values to build community.

Capture lessons learned to develop best practices.

Prompt action to change the company or organization.

Record the past to preserve corporate heritage.

Armed with these purposes and the stories that have already been shared and recorded, you will be able to convince the group that storytelling should be a daily occurrence.

Ten Ways to Become a Captivating Storyteller

People everywhere have one thing in common no matter their language or culture or location on the planet. We love to tell and be told stories.

Stories inform, entertain, grab peoples' attention and reflect their world to them for reflection and in so doing are valuable tools for teachers, speakers, parents and anyone else who wants to interact with others more effectively. Use them often and skillfully and watch people come alive in your presence.

Here are ten effective tips to make sure your stories are told well and captivate your listeners.

- Be on the lookout for stories throughout your day. Stories are everywhere so carry a notepad with you and jot the storyline down in point form. Flesh it out later. If you have a smartphone with a record capacity, you can use it to record any story ideas that come to you throughout your day.

- Know the story you are going to tell. When you know the storyline you can play with it to suit the audience. I find that I never tell the same story twice and that's the way it should be. The storyline remains the same, but the details can vary.

- Don't rush the story by speaking too quickly. Relax and enjoy the telling if it. It is your moment to shine. There are two temptations to avoid when telling your story, rushing and dragging it out. Be aware of your audience as you tell the story. Their body language will help you judge your storytelling pace.

- Don't be afraid to make it your own. You can add or subtract details and add texture and suspense with your voice, gestures and facial expressions. In short, you become an actor in your drama.

- Tell the story don't read it. Anyone can read a story not everyone can tell a story well. When you tell a story, you make a personal connection with the audience and can have the audience spellbound in no time.

- Use your voice for dramatic effect. It is the instrument you are going to use to establish mood, interest and emotion. If you tell your story in a monotonic voice, your audience will press their snooze button fast.

- Never let a story drag on and on. You want your story to be short and crisp and to the point.

- Don't get bogged down with detail. Keep to the storyline. You want to avoid the "Get on with it" response.

- Insert stories into general conversation whenever you get the chance. I heard the other day... I read in the paper recently about... I saw a man/woman in the coffee shop and... These are just a few of the many ways to insert your story into the conversation. It's great practice for you.

- Seldom explain your story to your listeners. Let the story speak for itself. There might be times when you can give a brief outline of the story lesson, but usually, it is best to let the story speak to the listener where they are in their life. Often the message you want them to get isn't the message they receive. Who is to say that the message they do receive isn't the one they were meant to.

When the situation is right, it is a bonus to get your audience involved in the telling of the story. This is especially true for speakers, teachers and presenters. You can have great fun with an interactive story. To get an idea of what I mean see the resource box below.

Become a Master Storyteller in Easy Steps

While reading an exhaustive book on the art of storytelling, I discovered a simple and profound truth buried in the final few chapters. It claims that stories will become new products. That one hit me right between the eyeballs. The implications are huge. The world has made a massive shift in the last few years. Value is no longer placed on what I can make, or even, what I know. My value is now entirely determined by my ability to weave my skills, knowledge, and life experiences into a compelling story. "Oh no," you may be thinking, "what's my story?" Here are some tips to help you develop your own story:

Pick a simple, classic story line from myths and fables. People like stories in which they already know the endings. Do you fancy yourself to be a hero, a princess, a champion of good over evil?

Pare the many details of your life down to the stuff that makes sense in the story. There's no need to spill your guts to the universe. People like stories where the hero/in struggles with something but always comes back to their true nature. For example, you are an honest worker who is faced with a temptation of theft, imagines all the things the stolen money could buy, but finally, decides to do the right thing.

Don't think that you are too boring to develop a great story. Some of the greatest myths have been about simple storylines. Read a few fables at the local book store and pick one that highlights the simple things of life.

Share the right juicy details. Only share secrets that help the development of the story and that you are comfortable sharing with everyone. Remember, word travels fast these days and once it's on the internet, it never dies. Ask yourself if you would feel comfortable having your children read this story before you hit the Publish button.

Write for babies. We're all little kids on the inside, and we want to hear how you have triumphed in big and small ways. Use words that are at an eighth-grade reading level to ensure that your audience can keep up with you.

Branch out into the business world. Practice writing a few personal stories first and then write couple for business. I can think of one person right now who landed a job interview while waiting for the kids at ballet class. You never know when you may need to present a story about your business life to land that next job.

Someone once said that your tattoo is the only thing you ever truly own. Sad? Profound? True? All three? To put a slightly more academic twist on it. Your knowledge is the only thing you ever truly own. And knowledge is useless without a way to share it with the world. Let's take it a little further: your story is the only thing you ever truly own. So then, you are going to need a story that shares your knowledge with the world, gives them an idea of who you are and why they should care.

Guidelines for Storytelling in Any Situation

Having a good sense of storytelling techniques is important for people involved in any form of communication. Unlike other ways to express a story, storytelling takes place at the moment between the storyteller and listener. It is a unique experience. Here are nine storytelling tips to use when you want to make the most of the story you have chosen.

1. Choose stories you like.

No matter if you are telling stories to children, illustrating a point in a business presentation or telling a sacred story in church or temple, use stories that you like. There are thousands upon thousands of stories in the world. Use the ones you like.

2. Practice your story.

Take the time to learn how to tell a story. Do not look at or hear a story just once and try to repeat it. Break the story into parts and remember the action piece by piece. Practice with a recording device and a gentle-yet-truthful friend who can hear your first attempts.

3. Take out the parts of the story that slow down the action.

Beginning storytellers will hear or read a story and then try to retell every nuance of the story. Storytelling occurs at the moment so not every detail has to be included each time. Ask yourself, "Do I need to tell this piece of the story this time? Is it critical to the story?"

4. Speak clearly.

If you have chosen a story you like, thought about the parts that fit and then practised telling that story, you will be confident of delivering it to the audience. Smile if the story requires it and then speak with that confidence. Enunciate and project your voice towards the listeners.

5. Keep an appropriate pace.

Again, with confidence in your own story and preparation, you will not be in a hurry to spill out the words of your story. Speak slowly enough to be understood but not so slowly that the minds of the audience go wandering.

6. Use a microphone.

You need to use a microphone to be heard. This shows respect to your audience. For experienced speakers, you will want a microphone if your group is 25 or more people. For those new to public-speaking, use the mic with any group larger than a few gathered around a table.

7. Keep good eye contact.

Look at your audience, linger with one person and move on to the next. It always amazes me how one fleeting moment of eye contact can make an audience member come to me and say, "I felt like you were talking to me personally."

8. Use natural gestures.

"You looked so confident up there. I never know what to do with my hands." When people say this to me, I am thankful that I took the time to prepare which gestures I would use and when I would use them. Make gestures that come naturally to you, but plan and prepare them ahead of time.

9. Avoid the "moral of the story" finishes.

Stories are often powerful pieces of Truth and storytelling is one of the most effective ways to convey them. You dilute the power of the story when you are the first to tell an audience what your story means. If you must do the "moral" of a story, ask your audience first to tell you what they think. It will surprise you.

Storytelling techniques like these nine can help you communicate better when you have a story to tell. If you are just starting, choose one or two of these storytelling tips that you will pay extra attention to in your next presentation.

Compelling Reasons to Tell Your Story

"We let ourselves loose on that simple blank piece of paper, and our bodies spill. The terror, the love... embodying our stories page after page. In a sense, the pen was our tongue; it is how we delineate the world." Coco J. Ginger

Your Story Can Help Others. Have you been through a life-altering experience? Have you survived something that others might face? Share what motivated you. Chances are you were inspired by someone else's story. Telling your story of perseverance and determination can encourage others to stay the course and forge ahead.

Your Story Can Teach A Life Lesson. Do you know the secret to do something better? Have you found a way to complete a task faster? Do you know a safer way to get a job done? Have you found an easier method for completing a repetitive job? Telling your story of survival or triumph can help others learn valuables lessons while avoiding costly mistakes.

Your Story Can Educate Others. Have you started a business? Did you master a challenging skill?

Have you overcome the (seemingly) impossible? Books are one of the fastest, easiest ways to teach a large contingency of people.

Your Story Can Inspire Others. Have you battled an illness? Have you raised a family? Perhaps you started a successful business or changed a life? Share that information. After all, just as iron sharpens iron, success inspires success.

Your Story Can Instruct Others. How-to books have been best sellers for years for a reason. Teaching others how to do what you do is a time-honoured tradition. Books and workbooks are great teaching tools and resource material.

Your Story Can Preserve Memories. From family history to church history, memories have been shared throughout the ages in the form of stories. Preserve your memories, experiences and laughter in a book. From family folklore to sermon collections to church history, a book is a permanent way to preserve memories and pictures.

Your Story Can Increase Your Business. Business owners and Professional Speakers can increase their income by up to 43% with a simple 100-page book. A book gets in front of people; you might not otherwise see; it brands you as an expert in your industry, and it opens two doors - one to your target market and one to other professionals in your industry. Professional Speakers with a back-of-the-room product create a whole new revenue stream.

www.ingramcontent.com/pod-product-compliance
Lightning Source LLC
Chambersburg PA
CBHW071810080526
44589CB00012B/739